IN THE HEADLINES

The Opioid Epidemic

TRACKING A CRISIS

THE NEW YORK TIMES EDITORIAL STAFF

Published in 2019 by New York Times Educational Publishing
in association with The Rosen Publishing Group, Inc.
29 East 21st Street, New York, NY 10010

First Edition

The New York Times
Alex Ward: Editorial Director, Book Development
Brenda Hutchings: Senior Photo Editor/Art Buyer
Phyllis Collazo: Photo Rights/Permissions Editor
Heidi Giovine: Administrative Manager

Rosen Publishing
Jacob R. Steinberg: Director of Content Development
Greg Tucker: Creative Director
Brian Garvey: Art Director
Michael Hessel-Mial: Editor

Cataloging-in-Publication Data
Names: New York Times Company.
Title: The opioid epidemic: tracking a crisis / edited by the New
York Times editorial staff.
Description: New York : The New York Times Educational Publish-
ing, 2019. | Series: In the headlines | Includes glossary and index.
Identifiers: ISBN 9781642820584 (pbk.) | ISBN 9781642820577
(library bound) | ISBN 9781642820560 (ebook)
Subjects: LCSH: Opioid abuse—Juvenile literature. | Drug
abuse—Juvenile literature. | Drug control—Juvenile literature. |
Opioid abuse—United States—Prevention.
Classification: LCC RC568.O45 O656 2019 | DDC 362.29'3—dc23

Manufactured in the United States of America

On the cover: Getty Images.

Contents

CHAPTER 2

Ripple Effects: Opioids, Heroin and Other Drugs

CHAPTER 3

The Business of Addiction Treatment

CHAPTER 4

Overprescription: Cause of the Crisis?

CHAPTER 5

The Response by Government and Law Enforcement

Introduction

IN THE EARLY years of this decade, news media began to report a sharp rise in addiction and overdose deaths caused by a dangerous class of drugs. Celebrities like football star Brett Favre and talk radio host Rush Limbaugh underwent highly publicized rehabilitation programs, and others like Michael Jackson and Prince died of overdoses. However, unlike other crises, the drugs in question were legal painkillers like oxycodone and hydrocodone. Previously restricted to post-operative and end-of-life medical care, their use dramatically expanded in the last two decades to become one of the most commonly prescribed medications. Today, the opioid epidemic is the worst drug crisis in American history, killing 64,000 people in 2017.

The crisis is systemic in its effects. A patient in chronic pain receives painkillers. That patient develops a tolerance and, finding heroin cheaper, turns to the illegal opioid. Additional synthetic opioids like fentanyl fill the economic niche created by increasing demand for illicit substances. Alarmed by the trends, doctors begin to restrict access to painkillers, driving additional vulnerable patients to turn to street drugs to meet their need. A wave of addiction sweeps the country, where in economically depressed areas the effects are devastating. Police are forced to practice emergency medicine in the field as they respond to overdose calls. Drug companies and treatment clinics, identifying a new market niche, begin selling addiction maintenance drugs that are themselves opioids; while helping many, these drugs also enter the illicit drug market. At the center of this conflicted tangle of government, medical treatment, law enforcement, legal and extralegal drug sales, are the families of people who have been impacted by addiction.

Noa Barreto, a recovering opioid addict, taking methadone in his home in Bay Ridge, Brooklyn, on a Sunday morning.

Part of the crisis begins with the honest desire to treat serious chronic pain. Since the 1990s, patient advocacy groups like the American Pain Foundation have advocated for expanded prescriptions of high-strength painkillers. However, many of these same organizations receive funding from pharmaceutical companies with financial stakes in the sale of opioids. Industry sales of opioids — as well as anti-overdose drugs like naloxone and new maintenance therapy drugs like buprenorphine and vivitrol — blur the lines between patient and profit.

The epidemic's most significant effect has been a change in public opinion on addiction. Comparable public health crises (like the rise of crack cocaine, or the AIDS epidemic) drew greater stigma due to association with racial and sexual minorities. With the opioid epidemic reaching veterans and suburban whites, addiction came closer to home and invited a more compassionate response. However, opioid addiction is not restricted to the affluent communities that appear in the headlines. Addiction rates in communities of color are as high or higher than their white counterparts.

In response to the crisis, communities most impacted have been forced to pioneer harm reduction strategies that the federal government then followed. And yet, the response by law enforcement remains conflicted. Many police departments, now accustomed to responding to overdoses and interacting with families affected, have chosen caretaker roles over merely jailing drug users. At the same time, supplies of cheap heroin and synthetic opioids from Mexico and China leave police scrambling to combat a quickly adapting market. Lastly, priorities of the Trump administration simultaneously seek to mitigate the crisis while returning to harsh punishments for drug users.

At the time of this writing, the opioid epidemic remains as dire as when the alarm bells were first sounded early in the decade. Because of the conflicting priorities of past and present administrations, there is great ambiguity in how the crisis will be addressed. What is certain is that the public understanding of addiction has changed, hitting closer to home in the dominant culture.

CHAPTER 1

The Opioid Epidemic's Human Impact

The articles in this chapter chronicle the devastation of addiction, which over the last decade have become a full-blown crisis. Some of the most devastating effects are in the rust belt, where the unemployment rate is high. More unexpected is the rate of addiction in middle and upper middle class households, in part due to the wide availability of legal painkillers. In addition to these groups, veterans experiencing chronic pain and post-traumatic stress disorder, as well as people of color, have fallen to addiction in large numbers.

Ohio County Losing Its Young to Painkillers' Grip

BY SABRINA TAVERNISE | APRIL 19, 2011

PORTSMOUTH, OHIO — This industrial town was once known for its shoes and its steel. But after decades of decline it has made a name for itself for a different reason: it is home to some of the highest rates of prescription drug overdoses in the state, and growing numbers of younger victims.

Their pictures hang in the front window of an empty department store, a makeshift memorial to more than two dozen lives. The youngest was still in high school.

Nearly 1 in 10 babies born last year in this Appalachian county tested positive for drugs. In January, police caught several junior high school students, including a seventh grader, with painkillers. Stepping Stone House, a residential rehabilitation clinic for women, takes patients as young as 18.

In Ohio, fatal overdoses more than quadrupled in the last decade, and by 2007 had surpassed car crashes as the leading cause of accidental death, according to the Department of Health.

The problem is so severe that Gov. John R. Kasich announced $36 million in new spending on it this month, an unusual step in this era of budget austerity. And on Tuesday, the Obama administration announced plans to fight prescription drug addiction nationally, noting that it was now killing more people than crack cocaine in the 1980s and heroin in the 1970s combined.

The pattern playing out here bears an eerie resemblance to some blighted cities of the 1980s: a generation of young people who were raised by their grandparents because their parents were addicts, and now they are addicts themselves.

"We're raising third and fourth generations of prescription drug abusers now," said Chief Charles Horner of the Portsmouth police, who often notes that more people died from overdoses in Ohio in 2008 and 2009 than in the World Trade Center attack in 2001.

"We should all be outraged," Chief Horner said. "It should be a No. 1 priority."

Scioto County, of which Portsmouth is the seat, has made it one, bringing what had been a very private problem out into the public.

A coroner and a pharmacist are among its state lawmakers, and a bill in the state legislature would more strictly regulate pain clinics where drugs are dispensed. The most popular drug among addicts here is the painkiller OxyContin.

The county's efforts got the attention of political leaders in the state, including Governor Kasich, who declared the county a pilot project for combating addiction.

A vast storefront has been transformed into a memorial to people who have died because of prescription drug abuse.

The problem is so bad that a storage company with business in the county recently complained to Chief Horner that it was having trouble finding enough job candidates who could pass drug tests.

"Around here, everyone has a kid who's addicted," said Lisa Roberts, a nurse who works for the Portsmouth Health Department. "It doesn't matter if you're a police chief, a judge or a Baptist preacher. It's kind of like a rite of passage."

About 10 years ago, when OxyContin first hurtled through the pretty hollow just north of town where the Mannering family lives, the two youngest children were still in high school. Their parents tried to protect them, pleading with neighbors who were selling the drug to stop. By mid-decade, they counted 11 houses on their country road that were dealing the drug (including a woman in her 70s called Granny), and their two youngest children, Nina and Chad, were addicted.

A vast majority of young people, officials said, get the drugs indirectly from dealers and other users who have access to prescriptions. Nina and Chad's father, Ed Mannering, said he caught a 74-year-old friend selling the pills from his front door. The sales were a supplement, the man said sheepishly, to his Social Security check.

"You drive down the road here, and you think, 'All these nice houses, no one's doing any of that stuff,' " said Judy Mannering, Nina and Chad's mother. "But they are. Oh, they are."

Nina Mannering tried to quit, her mother said. She had a small daughter to care for. She was in a counseling program for a few months, but was told to leave when her boyfriend brought her pills. At one point, Ms. Mannering counted the number of schoolmates in four graduating classes who had died from overdoses, her mother recalled. The total was 16.

"It's like being in the middle of a tornado," said Ed Hughes, director of the Counseling Center, a network of rehabilitation and drug counseling clinics in the county. "It was moving so fast that families were caught totally off guard. They had no idea what they were dealing with."

In January 2010, Ms. Mannering was killed less than a mile from her parents' house. A man broke into the house where she was staying with a 65-year-old veteran who had access to prescriptions, and shot them both, looking for pills, the police said. She was 29. Her daughter, who was 8 at the time, watched.

"It was like your worst fear that could ever come true," said Judy Mannering, who discovered her daughter's body at dusk, bathed in the light of a flickering, soundless television. Her son, Chad, served three years in prison for robbery. He is now sober.

Families are joining forces to combat the problem. Mothers whose children died from addiction have started to picket clinics that they believed were reckless with prescriptions. Last month the City Council passed a moratorium on new clinics.

"If you look at the problem, it's the darkest most malevolent thing you've ever seen," said Terry Johnson, a former Portsmouth coroner who is now a state assemblyman. "But right now, people are feeling like they are making a difference, and that's the most important thing. We need to capture that spirit."

The authorities have had some successes. Last month, agents raided a doctor's office and revoked his license. Another doctor from the area, Paul Volkman, is on trial in federal court in Cincinnati and accused of illegally disbursing prescription painkillers. But the drugs are legal, and it is hard to prosecute the people selling them. There are still five clinics in the county, several of them run by felons, officials said.

Chief Horner believes the problem will continue to fester without a coordinated effort by local, state and federal law enforcement agencies.

The state is stepping up efforts with prevention and rehabilitation, a spokeswoman for Governor Kasich said, but there are no plans to increase local financing for law enforcement, which remains, in the view of Chief Horner, woefully inadequate.

The trial of the man who shot Nina Mannering begins in June. Her mother awaits it with a mixture of dread and anticipation. For a while Judy Mannering felt so suffocated by grief that she could not leave the house, but that has passed.

Her grandchildren keep her going, as does her husband, Ed, a logger, who at 59 is still working full time, having spent their entire retirement savings on legal fees and rehab programs.

Mrs. Mannering has joined a group of other grieving mothers, who made the memorial of photographs in the store window. She has protested with them, holding up a sign with her daughter's photograph outside a clinic that dispenses pills. It was something she had never done before, but the ache of her loss gave her the courage.

"I miss her so much," she said of Nina. "If you had 100 kids, you'll never replace the one you've lost."

Some Veterans On Painkillers At Special Risk, A Study Finds

BY JAMES DAO | MARCH 8, 2012

VETERANS with post-traumatic stress disorder are more likely to be prescribed opioid pain killers than other veterans with pain problems and more likely to use the opioids in risky ways, according to a study published Wednesday by the Department of Veterans Affairs.

The study, published in the Journal of the American Medical Association, also found that veterans returning from Iraq and Afghanistan who were prescribed opioids for pain — and particularly those with post-traumatic stress disorder — had a higher prevalence of "adverse clinical outcomes," like overdoses, self-inflicted injuries and injuries caused by accidents or fighting.

The Department of Veterans Affairs and the Department of Defense have for years been trying to reduce the use of opioid pain therapy among active duty troops and veterans amid reports of overmedication, addiction, rampant drug abuse and accidental deaths caused by overdoses or toxic mixing of medications.

But the study raises new concerns that primary care doctors — the main prescribers of opioids to veterans — are not always following government guidelines intended to restrict opioid pain therapy for veterans with PTSD and other mental health diagnoses.

"There is often a big gulf between policies and practice," said Dr. Karen Seal, the director of an integrated care clinic at the San Francisco Veterans Affairs Medical Center who was the lead investigator on the study. "That is where the work needs to be done, in implementing policies and guidelines that are already there."

Dr. Robert D. Kerns, the national program director for pain management at the Department of Veterans Affairs, said in an interview that the department would draw attention to the new findings to push doctors to consider alternatives to opioid therapy, particularly with PTSD patients.

"This reinforces what's on the books and draws attention to an important challenge," Dr. Kerns said. "And it encourages us to continue to look for other innovations that can build on our existing initiatives."

Dr. Kerns said the veterans affairs medical system, as well as the Pentagon's health system, have been expanding alternative pain treatment programs to reduce the use of opioids, including acupuncture, chiropractic medicine, physical therapy, exercise therapy and relaxation techniques.

The veterans department is also looking to expand the use of psychological therapies already used for PTSD, mainly cognitive behavioral therapy, for treating chronic pain as well, said Dr. Kerns, who is himself leading research into that area.

Understanding the potential links between post-traumatic stress disorder and chronic pain is important because both are common among service members. By some estimates, one in five combat veterans report symptoms of PTSD, which can include nightmares, flashbacks, irritability and sleeplessness.

Chronic pain is also prevalent among troops and veterans, even those who have not experienced major battlefield injuries, like the loss of a limb. Lower back, knee, shoulder and other joint pains are common because of the routine physical stresses of the work, including wearing heavy body armor and packs.

Previous studies have shown that patients with post-traumatic stress disorder use opioid pain killers at higher rates than other patients. Dr. Seal said that one theory for the connection is that patients with anxiety disorders like PTSD may be more sensitive to pain.

"It's a vicious cycle," she said. "When you have an anxiety disorder, when you feel pain, you become anxious about it are more aware of it, and tend to complain about it."

She said most younger veterans tend to receive health care from primary care doctors who are not typically expert in handling post-traumatic stress disorder. But those doctors are trained to treat chronic pain, and many turn to opioids first because they want to relieve their patients' suffering quickly. The result, the study concluded, may be inappropriate prescriptions.

"Patient distress can drive potentially inappropriate opioid therapy, perhaps because physicians do not know how else to handle these challenging patients," the study said.

Dr. Seal said there were also studies suggesting that post-traumatic stress disorder disrupts the body's natural opiate system, which releases endorphins that reduce pain. The result is that people with PTSD may perceive pain at a lower threshold, she said.

The new study is considered particularly significant because of the sheer size of its sample: more than 141,000 veterans of Iraq and Afghanistan who received pain therapy for problems other than cancer from 2005 to 2010. Dr. Seal said the study was spurred in part by an article in The New York Times about troops and veterans who had died apparently from the toxic mixing of prescription medicines.

The researchers, most of them affiliated with the Department of Veterans Affairs, found that patients who had received mental health diagnoses were significantly more likely to receive opioid medication for pain than those without mental health problems. And veterans with post-traumatic stress disorder or a drug use disorder were the most likely to receive the prescriptions.

The researchers also looked at what they considered high-risk use of opioids, including high doses; using multiple types of opioids at one time; getting prescriptions for sedative hypnotics as well as opioids; and refilling opioid prescriptions early. Those actions could be indicators of drug abuse and addiction, as well as potential precursors for overdoses or toxic mixing of medications.

The study found that patients who had received mental health diagnoses showed patterns of higher-risk opioid use, and that the patterns were strongest among PTSD patients.

The researchers also found that veterans with post-traumatic stress disorder were more likely to receive opioid therapy even if they had known substance-use disorders, despite clear warnings that such prescriptions could be dangerous.

Dr. Seal said the researchers also found that more than four in 10 veterans with post-traumatic stress disorder were receiving opiates at the same time as benzodiazepines — a family of medications, including Xanax, that is prescribed for anxiety disorders like PTSD. Dr. Seal said the finding was "unsettling" because the mixing of opioids, benzodiazepines and alcohol could lead to respiratory depression and death.

But Dr. Seal, who treats many veterans with chronic pain problems in her clinic, said she was finding that more of her patients were willing to try alternative pain therapies.

"They know people who have had problems," she said. "They don't want to get hooked on narcotics. So there is great openness to treating pain with therapies other than opiates."

This is a more complete version of the story than the one that appeared in print.

Heroin Epidemic Increasingly Seeps Into Public View

BY KATHARINE Q. SEELYE | MARCH 6, 2016

CAMBRIDGE, MASS. — In Philadelphia last spring, a man riding a city bus at rush hour injected heroin into his hand, in full view of other passengers, including one who captured the scene on video.

In Cincinnati, a woman died in January after she and her husband overdosed in their baby's room at Cincinnati Children's Hospital Medical Center. The husband was found unconscious with a gun in his pocket, a syringe in his arm and needles strewn around the sink.

Here in Cambridge a few years ago, after several people overdosed in the bathrooms of a historic church, church officials reluctantly closed the bathrooms to the public.

"We weren't medically equipped or educated to handle overdoses, and we were desperately afraid we were going to have something happen that was way out of our reach," said the Rev. Joseph O. Robinson, rector of the church, Christ Church Cambridge.

With heroin cheap and widely available on city streets throughout the country, users are making their buys and shooting up as soon as they can, often in public places. Police officers are routinely finding drug users — unconscious or dead — in cars, in the bathrooms of fast-food restaurants, on mass transit and in parks, hospitals and libraries.

The visibility of drug users may be partly attributed to the nature of the epidemic, which has grown largely out of dependence on legal opioid painkillers and has spread to white, urban, suburban and rural areas.

Nationally, 125 people a day die from drug overdoses, 78 of them from heroin and painkillers, and many more are revived, brought back from the brink of death — often in full public view. The police in Upper

Darby, Pa., have even posted a video of another man shooting heroin on a public bus, and then being revived by Narcan, which reverses the effects of a heroin overdose, to demonstrate the drug's effectiveness.

Some addicts even seek out towns where emergency medical workers carry Narcan, "knowing if they do overdose, there's a good likelihood that when police respond, they'll be able to administer Narcan," said Special Agent Timothy Desmond, a spokesman for the New England region of the Drug Enforcement Administration.

In Linthicum, Md., Brian Knighton, a wrestler known as Axl Rotten in Extreme Championship Wrestling, died last month after overdosing in a McDonald's bathroom.

In Cincinnati in 2014, an Indiana couple overdosed on heroin at a McDonald's, collapsing in front of their children in the restaurant's play area.

In Niagara Falls, N.Y., a man was accused in October of leaving a 5-year-old boy unattended in a Dairy Queen while he went to the bathroom; he was later found on the floor with a syringe in his arm.

In Johnstown, Pa., a man overdosed on heroin on Feb. 19 in a bathroom at the Cambria County Library.

"Users need the fix as quickly as they can get it," said Edward James Walsh, chief of police in Taunton, Mass., a city 40 miles south of here that has been plagued with heroin overdoses in recent years. "The physical and psychological need is so great for an addict that they will use it at the earliest opportunity."

That reality has taxed law enforcement and city services across the country, and has stretched the tolerance of businesses that allow unfettered access to their bathrooms. Legal liability is an increasing worry.

"Overdosing has become an issue of great societal concern," said Martin W. Healy, chief legal counsel for the Massachusetts Bar Association. "I'm not aware of any seminal cases so far, but this is likely to be a developing area of the law."

After shooting up in public places, people often leave behind dirty needles, posing a health hazard. In response, some groups have called for supervised injection facilities, like those in Canada and Europe, where people can inject themselves under medical supervision. The goal is to keep them from overdosing and to curb infectious diseases. Such facilities are illegal in this country, although the mayor of Ithaca, N.Y., recently suggested opening one.

In Boston, where pedestrians step over drug users who are nodding off on a stretch of Massachusetts Avenue known as Methadone Mile, an organization for the homeless has planned what it calls a safe space, where users could ride out their high under supervision; it would not allow actual injection on site.

New England has been a cradle of the heroin epidemic. Middlesex County, which encompasses Cambridge, a city of 107,000 just west of Boston, has the highest number of overdose deaths from heroin and prescription pain pills in Massachusetts. From 2000 to 2014, Middlesex, which also includes the city of Lowell, a major heroin hotbed, had 1,634 opioid deaths.

No one keeps track of how many deaths occur in public spaces, but law enforcement officials agree the number is high.

"We quite frequently see folks using public areas," said Robert C. Haas, the Cambridge police commissioner.

It was the fear of someone dying in their bathrooms that led officials at Christ Church Cambridge to close public access to them in 2012. By doing so, the church did not experience the kind of tragic scenes that are occurring around the country, but the decision was difficult.

The church, which opened in 1761 and has a long history of social activism, had kept the bathrooms open to accommodate the homeless people around Harvard Square. But addicts were also using them. Closing them after decades of serving the public represented "a retreat from our ministry," Mr. Robinson said. But in consultation with the Cambridge police, the church reluctantly concluded that leaving the bathrooms open only enabled drug users.

Because there were no free-standing public toilets in Harvard Square, a popular shopping, culture and dining destination that is

The City of Cambridge spent $400,0000 to buy and install Harvard Square's first free-standing public toilet, which opened this month.

visited by eight million tourists a year, the absence of the church bathrooms was felt right away.

"Almost immediately, we began receiving calls saying, basically, 'What the hell just happened?' " said Denise Jillson, executive director of the Harvard Square Business Association. "They were saying, 'Our doorways and alleyways have become public urinals, and people are defecating everywhere.' "

After a campaign by business owners and local activists for a public toilet — which included stickers that read "I Love Toilets" and "Where Would Jesus Go?" — the City of Cambridge spent $400,000 to buy and install Harvard Square's first free-standing public toilet. It was unveiled on Feb. 12. Free to use and open 24 hours a day, it sits in a kiosk on a busy traffic island between the stately brick buildings of Harvard Yard and the weathered headstones in the Old Burying Ground, which dates to 1635.

The kiosk, called the Portland Loo and made in Oregon, was designed specifically to discourage drug use. It has slanted slats at the bottom that allow the police — or anyone — to peer in and see if someone has passed out on the concrete floor. It has no heat, air conditioning or noise insulation, all meant to foil anyone from getting too comfortable inside. The hand-washing faucet is outside, and an attendant cleans four times a day.

The outcome pleased Mr. Robinson, who said the anguishing decision to close the church bathrooms had "led to a broader response to the needs of the homeless in our neighborhood."

While the new toilet may improve life for some in Harvard Square, many restaurants, parking lots and other public spaces here and elsewhere remain potential sites for drug activity.

"Until we get a handle on the drug problem," said Capt. Timothy Crowley of the Lowell Police Department, "I think this is an issue we'll be dealing with for a long time."

A Death on Staten Island Highlights Heroin's Place in 'Mainstream Society'

BY MICHAEL WILSON | OCT. 2, 2016

THE MAN ENTERED the Red Robin restaurant inside the Staten Island Mall two minutes after 6 p.m. on a Friday. He walked straight past the booths and tables and entered the men's room.

A manager would find him there seven minutes later, lying on the floor with a needle and foaming at the mouth.

His name was Jonathan Ayers, 27, and he was declared dead within the hour that evening, Sept. 9, apparently of a heroin overdose.

Mr. Ayers's fatal overdose was the latest addition to a body count without precedent. So far in 2016, there have been 71 deaths that appear to be from heroin overdoses on the island, the Richmond County district attorney's office said, already on pace to more than double the record set two years ago. Nine people died of heroin overdoses in a recent 10-day period, prosecutors said.

Mr. Ayers left behind an account of his addiction. After his death, his mother, Ann Ayers, and brother, Christopher, found a journal he had kept for the last couple of years that chronicled the lies he had told them to conceal his continued dependence on drugs.

"I lie mostly I think because I am scared of being judged for the truth," Mr. Ayers wrote in May 2015. "This journal is where I tell the truth." Through the journal, his family would come to know the son and brother they had lost, and see the thoughts of a heroin addict.

Staten Island has been home to a heroin epidemic for several years, and it rivals the Bronx for the highest rate of deaths from heroin overdoses in New York City. The drug arrived to meet demand for opiates and fill the void left by law enforcement crackdowns on prescription pills, which were widely abused there.

Heroin, much cheaper than pills, became the drug of choice for the mostly white, middle-class neighborhoods on the island's south end. It was brought in bulk from other boroughs and New Jersey, and easily found on the island as an attractive diversion for bored and restless young people — creating a crisis for law enforcement, treatment programs and the parents of addicts, who have seen too many of their children end up in jail or the morgue.

Since 2010, the number of arrests on the island in which heroin or pills were found on the suspect has increased tenfold, to over 1,000 last year. Deaths attributed to heroin overdoses have also risen: In 2012 and 2013, the toll was 33 each year, and then jumped to 41 in 2014.

The deaths fall within a nationwide heroin epidemic that officials have compared to the onslaught of H.I.V. in the 1980s and 1990s. An estimated 125 people a day die from drug overdoses, 78 of them from heroin and pills. The rise in deaths has left virtually no corner of the country untouched, from New England to Appalachia to the Midwest and Southwest.

On Staten Island, the numbers could be far worse. Emergency medical workers and firefighters administered naloxone, an antidote to opioid overdoses, 89 times from January through July. Police officers have used it to save lives 35 times this year.

There have been new programs and initiatives and task forces and law enforcement operations and arrests. There have been infusions of funds. And yet nothing seems to be working.

"The drugs are too accessible and too acceptable," Michael McMahon, the Staten Island district attorney, said in an interview last month. "There seems to be a whole new population that thinks it's O.K. and not taboo."

Mr. McMahon said too few resources were being directed to the epidemic.

"If this many people were dying from Zika on Staten Island, we would have an all-out emergency crisis response to it," he said. "Anywhere else in the city of New York, if nine people died in 10 days from one

A page from the journal of Jonathan Ayers, 27, who died from an apparent heroin over-dose on Staten Island last month. Mr. Ayers wrote of his struggle with addiction, which he tried to hide from his family.

reason, it would be declared a citywide health emergency."

Mr. McMahon, shortly after taking office in January, announced the creation of the Overdose Response Initiative, with officers responding to every fatal overdose as if it were a homicide, gathering information on the victims and combing their cellphones for leads on the identity of the dealer of the drugs.

The investigations have given prosecutors and the police real-time data on overdoses; in the past, they had to wait for lengthy toxicology tests. The response has linked fatal overdoses to suspected dealers in two recent drug takedowns that led to 18 arrests.

Assistant Chief Edward Delatorre, the borough commander of Staten Island, said the police were initially led to believe that dealers had taken their own measure to avoid scrutiny — selling weaker heroin.

"We got word back that they were cautioning the other dealers who sold, 'Be careful what you sell on Staten Island,' " he said. "But here we are again in September with a surge."

Mr. McMahon believes that the recent string of deaths resulted not from a bad batch of heroin, but from the potency and ubiquity of the drug and the recklessness with which addicts are using it.

"What does that tell you, the death in the mall?" said Luke Nasta, the director of Camelot, an addiction treatment center on Staten Island. "It's part of mainstream society. Bright, shiny glass and nice stuff. The abundance of America, and using heroin and succumbing to an overdose. It's a crosscut of society. It's here. There's no denying it."

A CHRONICLED STRUGGLE

Mr. Ayers's overdose in the mall ended a struggle with addiction about which he wrote candidly in his journal while hiding it from his family. The journal and interviews with his family offer a glimpse of a middle-class addict seeming to hold his life together even as it spun downward.

"Have mercy on me, O Lord, for I am weak," Mr. Ayers, a Catholic, quoted from the Bible in one entry. "My bones are troubled."

Tall and stout at around 300 pounds, he was the classic gentle bear of a man, his family said. He graduated from Wagner College in 2010 with a degree in sociology but without solid plans, they said. Behind the scenes, his troubles had already begun.

"I had only been drinking, but when I started college I started smoking and eventually selling marijuana," Mr. Ayers wrote in 2015, according to a transcript of the journal provided by his brother. "It seemed harmless at first, but I guess it wasn't enough and I started to experiment." This led him to pills.

"And as the saying goes, 'That was that,' " he wrote. "It went from a weekend thing to a 3-day-a-week thing only at night and eventually to an everyday thing."

He traveled to his brother Christopher's home in Virginia in January 2015 to get away from the island. He stayed a month, attending church with his brother and sister-in-law, who were expecting a child, and discussing his troubles with his brother's pastor. But he also took mysterious drives to Baltimore, Christopher said last week. Asked why, Christopher said, Mr. Ayers told him he was visiting friends.

When Mr. Ayers returned to New York in February, his brother noticed $1,100 missing from his home, and he gave Mr. Ayers an ultimatum: Go to rehab or you'll never see your niece.

Mr. Ayers had been to an outpatient center on Staten Island, but had returned to pills, his family said. This time, he traveled to Florida for a three-week program.

Mr. Ayers's experiences were similar to those of many addicts on Staten Island. It is a widely held belief that one must leave the island to get clean.

"We can't just do the same old stuff we've been doing," said Diane Arneth, the president and chief executive of Community Health Action of Staten Island, a treatment center. "This really is an incredible crisis."

She said treatment centers have discussed identifying "crisis points" in an addict's downward spiral when they are open to the possibility of treatment, such as after an arrest or a visit to the emergency room, where they might meet with a counselor. "That's where people shift," she said.

Staten Island police officers see these crisis points every day, and they carry small containers of Narcan, a brand of naloxone, within easy reach in their pockets. Squirting it up the nose of an unconscious drug user blocks the absorption of opiates and stops an overdose. One officer, Crystal Vale, has saved three people with Narcan in the past year. "From being unable to respond, to being fully awake and not wanting to go to the hospital," she said last week.

She said she was present when a man was revived with Narcan, and when officers, paramedics and the man himself compared notes, they realized it was the third time he had been brought back from the brink — the Lazarus of Staten Island.

Another officer, Louise Sanfilippo, has logged 13 Narcan saves in a year and a half. She uses the antidote so often that she hurries to restock after a save, uncomfortable with an empty pocket.

"I never have none on me," she said.

The island lacks a 24-hour crisis center and relies on 9-to-5 offices to treat walk-in drug addicts looking for help. "People don't need help just during regular business hours," Ms. Arneth said.

'I'M SO SICK'

Mr. Ayers stayed clean after Florida, but not for long.

"I should have never went to that damn party. Even deleting all the numbers out of my phone didn't protect me from this," he wrote in April 2015. "I felt so ashamed and I wasted the past 50 days of my life and let everybody down who believed in me." He kept using: "I can't even look at my mom in the eye right now. All I do is ruin her life."

A year passed. He got a job at a bar. But his mother would come home from work at Wagner College and find him on the couch. " 'I'm so sick, I'm so sick,' " he told her, Ms. Ayers said. "He'd ask me for money for Suboxone," a prescribed drug that curbs opiate cravings, "and I gave it to him."

In August, he wrote his last journal entry: He needed to get his life together "or I'm going to end up in jail or worse dead."

On Thursday, Sept. 8, he said he had been to the doctor and that his prescription would be ready on Sept. 10.

On Sept. 9, his mother came home from work. He was on the couch. He asked a question that almost every mother of a certain age has heard before, practically a rite of passage.

Can I get a ride to the mall? He said he needed to meet a friend who had some extra Suboxone and was waiting at the massage chairs outside a Chase bank. "I don't know where that is," he told his mother.

She did. She drove him to the mall. He said he would be right back.

It is unclear exactly what Mr. Ayers did inside. But the massage chairs were right where he was told they would be, along with, his family assumes, what he came for. There he likely paused, figuring out a next move that would be his last, his mother waiting in the car outside, an escalator before him, the Red Robin below.

Drug Deaths in America Are Rising Faster Than Ever

BY JOSH KATZ | JUNE 5, 2017

AKRON, OHIO — Drug overdose deaths in 2016 most likely exceeded 59,000, the largest annual jump ever recorded in the United States, according to preliminary data compiled by The New York Times.

The death count is the latest consequence of an escalating public health crisis: opioid addiction, now made more deadly by an influx of illicitly manufactured fentanyl and similar drugs. Drug overdoses are now the leading cause of death among Americans under 50.

Although the data is preliminary, the Times's best estimate is that deaths rose 19 percent over the 52,404 recorded in 2015. And all evidence suggests the problem has continued to worsen in 2017.

Because drug deaths take a long time to certify, the Centers for Disease Control and Prevention will not be able to calculate final numbers until December. The Times compiled estimates for 2016 from hundreds of state health departments and county coroners and medical examiners. Together they represent data from states and counties that accounted for 76 percent of overdose deaths in 2015. They are a first look at the extent of the drug overdose epidemic last year, a detailed accounting of a modern plague.

The initial data points to large increases in drug overdose deaths in states along the East Coast, particularly Maryland, Florida, Pennsylvania and Maine. In Ohio, which filed a lawsuit last week accusing five drug companies of abetting the opioid epidemic, we estimate overdose deaths increased by more than 25 percent in 2016.

"Heroin is the devil's drug, man. It is," Cliff Parker said, sitting on a bench in Grace Park in Akron. Mr. Parker, 24, graduated from high school not too far from here, in nearby Copley, where he was a multisport athlete. In his senior year, he was a varsity wrestler and earned a scholarship to the University of Akron. Like his friends and teammates, he started using prescription painkillers at parties. It was fun, he said. By the time it stopped being fun, it was too late. Pills soon turned to heroin, and his life began slipping away from him.

Mr. Parker's story is familiar in the Akron area. From a distance, it would be easy to paint Akron — "Rubber Capital of the World" — as a stereotypical example of Rust Belt decay. But that's far from a complete picture. While manufacturing jobs have declined and the recovery from the 2008 recession has been slow, unemployment in Summit County, where Akron sits, is roughly in line with the United States as a whole. The Goodyear factories have been retooled into technology centers for research and polymer science. The city has begun to rebuild. But deaths from drug overdose here have skyrocketed.

In 2016, Summit County had 312 drug deaths, according to Gary Guenther, the county medical examiner's chief investigator — a 46 percent increase from 2015 and more than triple the 99 cases that went through the medical examiner's office just two years before. There were so many last year, Mr. Guenther said, that on three separate occasions the county had to request refrigerated trailers to store the bodies because they'd run out of space in the morgue.

It's not unique to Akron. Coroners' offices throughout the state are being overwhelmed.

In some Ohio counties, deaths from heroin have virtually disappeared. Instead, the culprit is fentanyl or one of its many analogues. In Montgomery County, home to Dayton, of the 100 drug overdose deaths recorded in January and February, only three people tested positive for heroin; 99 tested positive for fentanyl or an analogue.

Fentanyl isn't new. But over the past three years, it has been popping up in drug seizures across the country.

Most of the time, it's sold on the street as heroin, or drug traffickers use it to make cheap counterfeit prescription opioids. Fentanyls are showing up in cocaine as well, contributing to an increase in cocaine-related overdoses.

The most deadly of the fentanyl analogues is carfentanil, an elephant tranquilizer 5,000 times stronger than heroin. An amount smaller than a few grains of salt can be a lethal dose.

"July 5th, 2016 — that's the day carfentanil hit the streets of Akron," said Capt. Michael Shearer, the commander of the Narcotics Unit for the Akron Police Department. On that day, 17 people overdosed and one person died in a span of nine hours. Over the next six months, the county medical examiner recorded 140 overdose deaths of people testing positive for carfentanil. Just three years earlier, there were fewer than a hundred drug overdose deaths of any kind for the entire year.

This exponential growth in overdose deaths in 2016 didn't extend to all parts of the country. In some states in the western half of the U.S., our data suggests deaths may have leveled off or even declined. According to Dr. Dan Ciccarone, a professor of family and community medicine at the University of California, San Francisco, and an expert in heroin use in the United States, this geographic variation may reflect a historical divide in the nation's heroin market between the powdered heroin generally found east of the Mississippi River and the Mexican black tar heroin found to the west.

This divide may have kept deaths down in the West for now, but according to Dr. Ciccarone, there is little evidence of differences in the severity of opioid addiction or heroin use. If drug traffickers begin to shift production and distribution in the West from black tar to powdered heroin in large quantities, fentanyl will most likely come along with it, and deaths will rise.

First responders are finding that, with fentanyl and carfentanil, the overdoses can be so severe that multiple doses of naloxone — the anti-overdose medication that often goes by the brand name Narcan — are needed to pull people out. In Warren County in Ohio, Doyle Burke, the chief investigator at the county coroner's office, has been watching the number of drug deaths rise as the effectiveness of Narcan falls. "E.M.S.

crews are hitting them with 12, 13, 14 hits of Narcan with no effect," said Mr. Burke, likening a shot of Narcan to "a squirt gun in a house fire."

Early data from 2017 suggests that drug overdose deaths will continue to rise this year. It's the only aspect of American health, said Dr. Tom Frieden, the former director of the C.D.C., that is getting significantly worse. Over two million Americans are estimated to be dependent on opioids, and an additional 95 million used prescription painkillers in the past year — more than used tobacco. "This epidemic, it's got no face," said Chris Eisele, the president of the Warren County Fire Chiefs' Association and fire chief of Deerfield Township. The Narcotics Anonymous meetings here are populated by lawyers, accountants, young adults and teenagers who described comfortable middle-class upbringings.

Back in Akron, Mr. Parker has been clean for seven months, though he is still living on the streets. The ground of the park is littered with discarded needles, and many among the homeless here are current or former heroin users. Like most recovering from addiction, Mr. Parker needed several tries to get clean — six, by his count. The severity of opioid withdrawal means users rarely get clean unless they are determined and have treatment readily available. "No one wants their family to find them face down with a needle in their arm," Mr. Parker said. "But no one stops until they're ready."

ABOUT THE DATA

Our count of drug overdoses for 2016 is an estimate. A precise number of drug overdose deaths will not be available until December.

As the chief of the Mortality Statistics Branch of the National Center for Health Statistics at the C.D.C., Robert Anderson oversees the collection and codification of the nation's mortality data. He noted that toxicology results, which are necessary to assign a cause of death, can take three to six months or longer. "It's frustrating, because we really do want to track this stuff," he said, describing how timely data on cause of death would let public health workers allocate resources in the right places.

To come up with our count, we contacted state health departments in all 50 states, in addition to the District of Columbia, asking for their statistics on drug overdose deaths among residents. In states that didn't have numbers available, we turned to county medical examiners and coroners' offices. In some cases, partial results were extrapolated through the end of the year to get estimates for 2016.

While noting the difficulty of making predictions, Mr. Anderson reviewed The Times's estimates and said they seemed reasonable. The overdose death rate reported by the N.C.H.S. provisional estimates for the first half of 2016 would imply a total of 59,779 overdose deaths, if the death rate remains flat through the second half of the year. Based on our reporting, we believe this rate increased.

While the process in each state varies slightly, death certificates are usually first filled out by a coroner, medical examiner or attending physician. These death certificates are then collected by state health departments and sent to the N.C.H.S., which assigns what's called an ICD-10 code to each death. This code specifies the underlying cause of death, and it's what determines whether a death is classified as a drug overdose.

Sometimes, the cases are straightforward; other times, it's not so easy. The people in charge of coding each death — called nosologists — have to differentiate between deaths due to drug overdose and those due to the long-term effects of drug abuse, which get a different code. (There were 2,573 such deaths in 2015.) When alcohol and drugs are both present, they must specify which of the two was the underlying cause. If it's alcohol, it's not a "drug overdose" under the commonly used definition. Ideally, every medical examiner, coroner and attending physician would fill out death certificates with perfect consistency, but there are often variations from jurisdiction to jurisdiction that can introduce inconsistencies to the data.

'The Pills Are Everywhere': How the Opioid Crisis Claims Its Youngest Victims

BY JULIE TURKEWITZ | SEPT. 20, 2017

WHEN PENNY MAE CORMANI died in Utah, her family sang Mormon hymns — "Be Still My Soul" — and lowered her small coffin into the earth. The latest victim of a drug epidemic that is now taking 60,000 lives a year, Penny was just 1.

Increasingly, parents and the police are encountering toddlers and young children unconscious or dead after consuming an adult's opioids.

At the children's hospital in Dayton, Ohio, accidental ingestions have more than doubled, to some 200 intoxications a year, with tiny bodies found laced by drugs like fentanyl. In Milwaukee, eight children have died of opioid poisoning since late 2015, all from legal substances like methadone and oxycodone. In Salt Lake City, one emergency doctor recently revived four overdosing toddlers in a night, a phenomenon she called both new and alarming.

"It's a cancer," said Mauria Leydsman, Penny's grandmother, of the nation's opioid problem, "with tendrils that are going everywhere."

While these deaths represent a small fraction of the epidemic's toll, they are an indication of how deeply the American addiction crisis has cut.

And communities from Appalachia to the Rocky Mountains and beyond are feeling its effects at all ages. In August, in the latest sign of the direness of the situation, President Trump said he would declare the opioid crisis a national emergency, a move that could allow cities and states to access federal disaster relief funds.

Eighty-seven children died of opioid intoxication in 2015, according to the Centers for Disease Control and Prevention, up from just 16 in

The infant section of the Lehi City Cemetery in Utah, where Penny Mae Cormani, a toddler who died after ingesting heroin, is buried.

1999. By comparison, gunshot wounds kill four or five times as many children each year.

But at hospitals like Primary Children's in Utah, drug overdoses now outstrip gun injuries among young people.

"There are no pill parties happening in preschools," said Dr. Jennifer Plumb, the emergency doctor who recently treated four opioid-sick toddlers in a night. "These kids aren't making a choice because they are trying to get high on a substance. It's that the pills are everywhere."

Unlike infants born with addiction, these children are coming across heroin and other drugs in the days and years after birth.

In Philadelphia this summer, a 9-month-old rolled onto a needle while in bed with her father. Kyleeh Isabella Mazaba, 20 months, died after drinking methadone left in a water bottle in the family van. James Lionel Vessell Jr., 2, swallowed oxycodone pills he found in a purse on his mother's bed. And in early August, Kentucky officials treated an infant and three emergency responders believed to have been sickened by carfentanil-laced heroin that traveled through the air.

Often, emergency responders attempt to revive children with Narcan, an overdose reversal drug that works on small bodies as well as large ones.

Then come the questions for investigators. How did the substance get there? How did the child find it? Can this be stopped?

Sometimes officials charge caretakers with neglect or manslaughter. In one case this year, the authorities accused a couple of child endangerment after they admitted to rubbing Suboxone on their daughter's gums, an attempt to hide the fact that she was born with an addiction.

But often the details go undiscovered, with witnesses too young to offer their own accounts.

Penny Mae Cormani was born Nov. 12, 2014, to Cassandra Leydsman and Casey Cormani, both mired in addiction. A year later, while the three of them were staying with another couple, Penny ingested enough heroin to kill a grown man.

Ms. Leydsman, the grandmother, said she believes Penny was scooting around on the floor during breakfast and found a bit of heroin, eating it like any child would. The official record is silent on exactly how the infant found the substance. But Penny's parents pleaded guilty to third-degree felonies — Cassandra to child abuse homicide and Casey to attempted manslaughter — and went to prison.

Cassandra Leydsman is likely to serve 36 months.

Ms. Leydsman, 68, is a devout Mormon who raised five children with her husband, a retired pharmaceuticals manager. She traced her daughter's addiction back more than a decade, to a car accident that prompted a doctor to prescribe OxyContin.

This led to a pill addiction that led to a heroin addiction that ultimately ended in Penny's death. The family buried Penny in a baby cemetery south of Salt Lake City. Ms. Leydsman visits regularly, bringing with her holiday decorations, balloons and soft toys. In prison, Cassandra is receiving drug treatment.

"She knows she's responsible," Ms. Leydsman said of her daughter. "And it's a terrible burden to go around knowing you're responsible for the death of your child."

In Utah, most opioid overdoses at the state's only children's hospital involve buprenorphine, oxycodone, methadone and hydrocodone, and Dr. Plumb attributes the problem to the state's continued dependence on legal painkillers.

In a state of three million people, pharmacists fill some 7,200 opioid prescriptions a day, according to 2015 data. Curious toddlers, Dr. Plumb said, are finding mom's Suboxone strip, grandpa's OxyContin.

In Montgomery County, Ohio, which includes Dayton, the story is different.

Drug peddlers have flooded the community with fentanyl, a legal synthetic used for extreme pain, and powerful analogues like carfentanil, a substance 5,000 times stronger than heroin.

Inhaling, touching or ingesting a carfentanil dose smaller than a few grains of salt can be lethal. Dr. Kelly Liker, the medical director for child advocacy at Dayton Children's Hospital, attributes a growing number of child overdoses to the rise of these substances.

In September of last year, Lee L. Hayes, 2, died in Montgomery County of fentanyl intoxication. In April, Nathan L. Wylie, 13, died of similar poisoning. And in May, Mari'onna Allen, 1, fatally overdosed in her grandmother's home on Dayton's East Fifth Street.

"It's a disgrace that kids have to be subject to this," said Mari'onna's great-grandmother, who declined to give her name. "They're innocent, they don't have a clue, and they don't know drugs from candy."

The Bronx's Quiet, Brutal War With Opioids

BY JOSE A. DEL REAL | OCT. 12, 2017

THE BODIES TURN UP in public restrooms, in parks and under bridges, skin tone ashen or shades of blue. The deceased can go undiscovered, sometimes for hours, or days if they were alone when they injected heroin and overdosed.

Terrell Jones, a longtime resident of the Bronx, was pointing to the locations where overdoses occurred as he drove through the East Tremont neighborhood, the car passing small convenience stores, row-houses and schools.

"This is sometimes where people are being found, in their houses, dead," said Mr. Jones, 61, looking toward a housing project along 180th Street. "Especially in the South Bronx, you have so many people in housing who overdose. To actually sit there and witness this whole thing? You're watching this person turn all different colors. You know what I'm saying?"

The dramatic rise in opioid-related deaths has devastated communities around the United States in recent years, and has stirred concern among law enforcement and public health officials alike in New York City.

Here, the reports about the epidemic and its ravages have mostly centered on Staten Island, where the rate of deaths per person is the highest of the five boroughs. But perhaps nowhere in the city has the trajectory of opioid addiction been as complex as in the Bronx, where overdose deaths were declining until a new surge began at the turn of the decade, and where more residents are lost to overdoses than anywhere else in the city. On Bronx streets, the epidemic's devastation is next door, down the street, all around.

The increase in deaths — now at the highest levels since the city began collecting the data in 2000 — has been fueled by social forces

Two outreach workers, Clara Cardelle and Mike Bailey, approach a man using heroin in Tremont Park in the Bronx in September.

that have left some Bronx residents especially vulnerable: a history of high drug use in the area; a growing supply of cheap heroin on the streets; and the proliferation of a deadly synthetic opioid, fentanyl.

Mr. Jones said he never leaves his apartment in Hunts Point without a dose of naloxone, a medication that can be used to reverse opioid overdoses. The antidote — whose brand name is Narcan — has become a necessary stopgap to prevent deaths that happen in public spaces. Mr. Jones, who has himself struggled with drug addiction in the past, now works with the New York Harm Reduction Educators to help drug users.

"Regardless of how they died, it wasn't an intentional death. Nobody woke up and said, 'Today I want to die of an overdose,' " he said. "People have issues and reasons they're using drugs, and it's not for us to judge."

In 2016, 1,374 people died from overdoses in New York City, up from 937 in 2015, according to the New York City Office of Chief Medical Examiner. The vast majority of those lethal overdoses involved opioids, a drug classification comprising prescription painkillers like Oxycodone and Percocet, morphine, and the illegal street counterpart, heroin. An additional 344 overdose deaths were reported across the city from January to March of this year, according to preliminary data made available by the New York City Health Department.

More Bronx residents died of drug overdoses in 2016 than any other New York City borough — 308. That's more than double the number in 2010, 128. Fatal overdoses in the borough are now at their highest rates since at least 2000, as far back as official data is available. Eighty-five percent of those deaths involved opioids, and about 76 percent involved heroin or fentanyl specifically.

Of the five neighborhoods with the highest opioid-related overdose rates in 2015 and 2016, four were in the Bronx — Hunts Point-Mott Haven, Crotona-Tremont, High Bridge-Morrisania and Fordham-Bronx Park — and one was in Staten Island, South Beach/Tottenville.

The crisis in the Bronx stems, at least in part, from a surge of opioids in a place where some residents have long struggled with addiction. Heroin has become much cheaper in recent years as the supply in the United States has grown, according to the Office of the Special Narcotics Prosecutor for the City of New York, and individuals with histories of drug abuse are particularly vulnerable to relapse amid a surge of cheap drugs. It has also become significantly more potent.

The cheaper, stronger heroin has been made even more dangerous by the proliferation of fentanyl, which is 50 times more powerful than heroin. Interviews with nearly 200 drug users conducted by the city health department suggest that most users are not directly seeking fentanyl; narcotics experts say the drug is likely being mixed into heroin batches, often without the dealers themselves knowing, let alone users. As effective as naloxone can be in reversing overdoses and restoring breathing, fentanyl overdoses are often too extreme for the antidote to work. And naloxone is ultimately a Band-Aid to a broader, systemic addiction crisis across the city.

"In a place like the Bronx, where there was a long term underlying addiction issue, all of a sudden you saturate the area with cheap accessible heroin, and you're going to start to see the spike," the city's special narcotics prosecutor, Bridget Brennan, said in an interview.

The recent surge of illegal heroin in the Bronx in many ways mirrors the surge of prescription painkillers that fueled the opioid epidemic in suburban and rural communities. In the Bronx, as elsewhere, accessibility is related to spikes in consumption and addiction.

An illegal prescription painkiller market also thrived in the Bronx. In one high-profile case, a physician who owned several medical clinics in the Bronx was convicted of illegally distributing millions of prescription painkillers between 2011 and 2014. (Oxycodone from that "pill mill" was likely distributed in the Bronx, northern parts of Manhattan and Brooklyn, officials have said.)

In Staten Island, the proliferation of prescription painkillers — often acquired illicitly through friends or dealers — led to an explosion in overdose deaths earlier this decade. Eventually Staten Island itself developed a market for heroin dealers.

"This group of people in Staten Island, who might have been put off by the illegality of heroin, they're already addicted" to opioids, Ms. Brennan said, and were therefore more willing to try it. The ensuing rise in opioid-related deaths among white, middle-class men and women has helped change popular conceptions about who is susceptible to drug addiction.

"The impact plays out differently in different parts of the city, and different parts of the country, depending on the historical arch. But it's got a huge impact wherever it hits. It's so cheap, so accessible, so pure," explained Ms. Brennan.

Given the significantly larger overall numbers of deaths in the Bronx, Dr. Chinazo Cunningham, a primary care physician affiliated with Montefiore Medical Center who has worked in the Bronx for

A van operated by the Washington Heights Corner Project and New York Harm Reduction Educators provides training in the Bronx for the use of naloxone, a medication that can be used to reverse opioid overdoses.

decades, lamented that opioid-related deaths in the borough have not received more attention. She said the interest in Staten Island likely stems from its relatively new addiction crisis and the fact that white middle-class residents are being affected.

"Really, the reason we care about the opioid epidemic is because it's affecting populations that are white and affluent," she said. "The way that we got to this is bittersweet, that this is what it has taken to shift the conversation to this way we're talking about it."

Dr. Cunningham, who is certified in addiction medicine, said it is important to balance medical data against stereotypes "portraying everyone in the Bronx as a drug user, or suggesting that all brown people are drug users." Such assumptions are partially to blame for apathy in the overdose death crisis in the borough, she said.

In fact, in 2016, the highest rate of overdose deaths in the Bronx was among white residents, followed by Hispanics, and then African-

Americans. Just 9 percent of Bronx residents are classified as non-Hispanic white.

City Hall has acknowledged the high death count in the Bronx, and has pledged a broad, citywide program to drive down fatalities. In March, Mayor Bill de Blasio chose Lincoln Hospital in the South Bronx to announce the new effort. Calling the 2016 fatalities "shocking" and "a wake up call," Mr. de Blasio committed $38 million a year to an initiative aimed at reducing fatal drug overdoses by 35 percent over five years; he vowed to dramatically expand government-funded naloxone distribution throughout the city, while expanding treatment options and reducing the supply of opioids.

But community organizations on the ground and law enforcement are still struggling to curb the number of fentanyl- and heroin-related deaths.

On a Wednesday afternoon in September, a plain gray van was parked across the street from Tremont Park, on the corner of Arthur and Tremont Avenues, and a blue tarp was erected next to it. The arrangement was a perhaps modest, but nonetheless crucial, outpost in the fight against opioid-related overdose deaths in the Bronx. Throughout the year, from this makeshift bureau and several others in the borough, Mr. Jones and his colleagues at the New York Harm Reduction Educators hand out information about opioid deaths, offer free naloxone, and operate a syringe exchange program. (The program is funded largely through government grants.)

Adriana Pericchi sat in the blue tent, training passers-by how to administer naloxone to someone suffering an overdose. Slipping back and forth between conversational Spanish and English with a man seeking naloxone and fentanyl test strips, she moved methodically step-by-step, beginning with an overview of the physical symptoms of overdose: blue nails or lips, skin discoloration and shallow breaths. She jammed naloxone into a test dummy's nose before playacting chest compressions and rescue breathing.

"First the breathing stops, then the brain, then the heart," Ms. Pericchi reminded the man, a heroin user, who nodded along.

Later, sitting in a nearby McDonald's, Ms. Pericchi opened up about the emotional toll felt by her colleagues at Washington Heights Corner Project and other organizations in the field.

"A lot of us are doing our best, but it's just not enough, it's not enough," she said. "You're mourning for one particular person who you knew and loved. And really quickly that avalanches into mourning for the state of the city, the state, the country."

Mr. Jones said the Bronx needs more resources to combat heroin deaths, and blamed racial politics for insufficient resources. He said policies from the War on Drugs have also made community members distrustful of the police. Speaking softly and slowly, he disclosed that he sold drugs during the 1980s to support his crack habit, eventually serving more than two years in prison.

Now, decades later, as he devotes himself to helping drug users who need help, Mr. Jones sees a continued double standard for Bronx residents, who are stripped of compassion and dignity amid an epidemic that has engendered sympathy and panic in other communities.

From his vantage point, the attitude toward the opioid deaths today is still influenced by racialized attitudes about the crack and heroin epidemics before.

"It's just color. It's like we're part of a third-world country because we're not part of the so-called privileged people," Mr. Jones said. "I could be wrong, but I'm saying that it's because of our color. It's a big issue."

A Foster Child of the Opioid Epidemic

BY LISA MARIE BASILE | NOV. 24, 2017

I SAT ON A wrought iron daybed facing an open window, and a warm breeze was pooling in. It was the first day in my second foster home. The room was made up to seem welcoming, but its pleasantness somehow felt oppressive. I felt dirty, worthless and consumed by fear.

I was about to start 10th grade for the second time, since I'd failed the year before. Earlier that morning, I said goodbye to my 10-year-old brother, helped him into a car, and watched him ride away to live with another foster family.

"Go ahead and hang up your clothes," my new foster mother said. Sternness was her way of normalizing an abnormal situation. I was abnormal. I came from abnormal. None of my clothes were really hang-up-able. I felt I had to apologize for my clothes, for my parents, for myself.

Both of my parents had used drugs — opioids — since my childhood. I'm 8: My mother locks my screaming, doped-up father out. I'm crying on the other side of a door as she commands me not to open it. I'm 12: This time I'm banging on a door as my mother locks herself into a public bathroom to get high. Those memories stay sharp. It wasn't always like this, though. We once lived in a sunny apartment in New Jersey; my mom braided my hair, kissed me a hundred times, comforted me when I was sad or sick.

My father, an accomplished blues guitarist, let me stay up late and watch horror movies with him. He let my creativity blossom.

My father struggled with addiction first — he went to rehab and to prison and, for the most part, exited our lives. My mother's addiction came later, in my early teens. With limited resources, my parents didn't have the option to quit their jobs and check themselves into long-term rehab. Addiction poisoned everything.

In eighth grade, I spent Christmas in a 10x10 room in a homeless shelter with my mother, brother and a bunk bed. We were spoiled with donated gifts. I'd gotten a Tamagotchi — a small digital "pet" I could care for. I'd feed it and clean it and watch it grow, and, despite it being childish, having that responsibility brought me a sense of stability. My mother wept as we opened the presents. She gave us a few things, too: She wrapped socks in sparkly ribbons and gave me a lacy green shirt that I wore to shreds.

The next morning, we walked with our mother to a nearby methadone clinic. My brother carried his favorite gift: a small blue train with silver wheels.

Eventually, the state took us away. My mother just couldn't get better or take care of us properly, they believed.

The couple who became my foster parents for my high school years gave me a good home and access to an incredible school system, but I still would rather have been with my mother. Unlike my foster parents, she understood me on a deep level. There was no way my foster parents could truly know me, I thought. I kept them at a distance; we were just different.

In school, I crafted an image of "happy," repressing the heaviness that hung on me. My teachers treated me with a softness and patience that I needed, but they also pushed me hard; they wanted me to go to college, to transcend my life.

I purposely didn't make friends in my new high school. I didn't want anyone to know where my house was or why I lived with strangers. Some of them found out, I think, and they wrote me off as a freak. I felt invisible, but I didn't try to fight it.

I wish I'd had relatives to live with or at least communicate with at the time but my grandmother was in Virginia, and she was dying. The stigma of addiction kept other relatives at bay. Years later, only one of them apologized.

I missed the way my mother would blast Led Zeppelin or Pink Floyd while cleaning the house. She loved watching design TV shows and making plans for her dream home.

Despite her struggle, she was kind and hopeful and light — and I needed that light. I missed my brother, too. Even though he was younger than me, we were similar; we made the same jokes, we thought in similar ways, and we'd been through the same pain.

Still, I was one of the lucky ones. My parents didn't die from an overdose and I wasn't abused or neglected by my foster parents — unlike so many other foster kids. If I was lucky, then what does that mean for the others?

By the time I finished high school, my mother had gotten clean. She'd maintained sobriety, gotten a job and rented a small, lopsided house in the woods of rural New Jersey. It was the most beautiful house I could imagine, despite its old walls and slanted roof and barely working furnace.

The first time she hugged me, I stayed close in her arms, listening to the sounds of birds outside.

I stayed with her briefly before starting college in the following weeks. It was painful saying goodbye yet again, but this time, I knew where she was and I could go back. I had a chance to get beyond all of this, and I wanted to take it.

My mom decorated the house in whites and tans. She bought cheap things but made them look stunning. You could sense her self-care in every chair, every carpet, every curtain.

At night in the summer, she'd make salad with cucumbers from the farmers' market and we'd watch the fireflies. Then, we'd sit and drink coffee on our deck while a thousand cicadas sang. Coming home to see her was a quiet healing; every time I came back to that house, I was less sad, less lost.

She's since moved, but that place in the woods remains a powerful symbol of rebirth.

And while it took years for me to speak with my father again, I do now. He's still a musician, he fishes in a green boat, and he lives a simple life. I can sense their shame and regret; when it comes up, that much is clear, but we don't talk about it often. They both agreed that I could write about our experience; they say it's my story and I may tell it.

Addiction is an indiscriminate disease. You want to blame the weakness inside a person. But like a tree, it extends its gnarled branches in many directions: toward the children it hurts, toward the state it burdens and toward the victims it consumes.

There is a space inside me that is still filled with shame, embarrassment, fear, anger, resentment and — as I get older — a need to tell this truth, to get this ugliness out of me.

In the end, though — and as I grow older — I hold to one thing: compassion. Strangers had an audacious compassion for my mother and father, and my foster parents and schoolteachers had an unwavering compassion for me. I carry that compassion with me each day — it is as vital to me as blood and air, and it colors my entire life.

The Opioid Crisis Is Getting Worse — Particularly for Black Americans

BY JOSH KATZ AND ABBY GOODNOUGH | DEC. 22, 2017

THE EPIDEMIC OF drug overdoses, often perceived as a largely white rural problem, made striking inroads among black Americans last year — particularly in urban counties where fentanyl has become widespread.

Although the steep rise in 2016 drug deaths has been noted previously, these are the first numbers from the Centers for Disease Control and Prevention to break down 2016 mortality along geographic and racial lines. They reveal that the drug death rate is rising most steeply among blacks, with those between the ages of 45 and 64 among the hardest hit.

Drug deaths among blacks in urban counties rose by 41 percent in 2016, far outpacing any other racial or ethnic group. In those same counties, the drug death rate among whites rose by 19 percent. The data, released on Thursday, suggests that the common perception of the epidemic as an almost entirely white problem rooted in overprescription of painkillers is no longer accurate, as fentanyl, often stealthily, invades broader swaths of the country and its population.

Driven by the continued surge in drug deaths, life expectancy in the United States dropped for the second year in a row last year. It's the first consecutive decline in national life expectancy since 1963. Drug overdoses have now surpassed heart disease as the leading cause of death for Americans under the age of 55.

In Washington, D.C., the emergence of fentanyls caused the rate of drug deaths to double in a single year. The rate of drug deaths there is now on par with those in Ohio and New Hampshire. It's an unsurprising consequence of an epidemic that is both widespread and extremely localized. If fentanyls enter the drug supply in one area, deaths can

Terrell Jones, left, and his colleagues at the New York Harm Reduction Educators hand out information about opioid deaths, offer free naloxone, and operate a syringe exchange program.

accumulate rapidly. Drug deaths are also up sharply in cities like St. Louis, Baltimore, Philadelphia and Jacksonville, Fla.

Dr. Andrew Kolodny, the co-director of opioid policy research at Brandeis University's Heller School for Social Policy and Management, said it appeared that many of the African-Americans who died were older men who had become addicted to heroin during a previous epidemic in the 1970s. "Despite beating the odds for the past 40 to 50 years," he said, "they're dying because the heroin supply has never been so dangerous — increasingly it's got fentanyl in it or it's just fentanyl sold as heroin."

Fentanyl-laced cocaine, too, may be playing a role. A study published this month in the journal Annals of Internal Medicine found that cocaine-related overdose deaths were nearly as common among black men between 2012 and 2015 as deaths due to prescription opioids in white men over the same period. Cocaine-related deaths were slightly more common in black women during that period than deaths due to heroin among white women, according to the study. But it also found that the largest recent increases in overdose deaths among blacks were attributed to heroin. One of the researchers, David Thomas of the National Institute on Drug Abuse, said he did not know whether some of the cocaine-attributed deaths in the study involved fentanyl, although he had heard anecdotally of such mixing.

The study, by researchers at the National Cancer Institute and the National Institute on Drug Abuse, also found that the recent rise in overdose death rates was sharpest among older blacks. The same held true last year in New York City.

"What's really interesting is you're not seeing younger blacks getting involved in heroin as much," said Denise Paone, senior director of research and surveillance in the city's Bureau of Alcohol and Drug Use Prevention.

Across the board, though, fentanyl has caused a huge spike in overdose deaths in New York in just the last year. Fentanyl played a role in about 16 percent of overdose deaths in 2015 and 44 percent in 2016, Dr. Paone said, compared with 3 percent in prior years. A growing number of the deaths involve cocaine cut with fentanyl, she added — which is probably particularly deadly for someone who has not used opioids before.

In Ohio, which had the nation's second-highest overdose rate last year, the medical examiner in Cuyahoga County told a United States Senate subcommittee in May that a fast-rising rate of fentanyl-related deaths among blacks was probably a result of drug dealers mixing fentanyl with cocaine. In Cuyahoga County (the home of Cleveland), fentanyl contributed to the deaths of five African-Americans in 2014, 25 in 2015 and 58 in 2016. But both opioids and cocaine still kill far more whites than blacks there.

Brandon Marshall, an associate professor of epidemiology at the Brown University School of Public Health, said it was hard to sort out how many deaths involved people taking cocaine cut with fentanyl versus people who died of an opioid overdose but also happened to have cocaine in their blood at the time.

Dr. Kolodny said he believes the latter is more common. "Many people who are overdosing because of an extremely dangerous heroin supply also use other drugs," he said, "so I think the cocaine is sort of an incidental finding."

Health experts say the evolving nature of the crisis suggests that progress against it will be slow, despite stepped-up efforts to address it with medication-assisted treatment and naloxone, which can save people who have overdosed. As overdose deaths keep climbing, there is a good chance that life expectancy will be found to have declined again this year, said Robert Anderson, chief of the mortality statistics branch of the National Center for Health Statistics. If so, it would be the first three-year period of consecutive life expectancy declines since World War I and the Spanish flu pandemic in 1918.

Dr. Kolodny pointed to the rising drug death rate among older black men, many of whom he said have probably used heroin on and off since the 1970s, as evidence that progress against the new epidemic could take decades.

"Forty, 50 years later we're still paying a price," he said. "What this means is for our current epidemic, we're going to be paying a very heavy human and economic price for the rest of our lives."

CHAPTER 2

Ripple Effects: Opioids, Heroin and Other Drugs

The opioid crisis is not limited to a single drug, legal or otherwise. In many cases, addiction to prescription pain-killers has spiraled into increased rates of addiction to heroin and other drugs. With increasing frequency, users choose heroin as a cheaper alternative to commercial opioids. In addition, synthetic opioids like fentanyl have become unexpected additives to other drugs — and a major cause of overdoses.

Prescription Painkillers Seen as a Gateway to Heroin

BY BENEDICT CAREY | FEB. 10, 2014

THE LIFE OF a heroin addict is not the same as it was 20 years ago, and the biggest reason is what some doctors call "heroin lite": prescription opiates. These medications are more available than ever, and reliably whet an appetite that, once formed, never entirely fades.

Details are still emerging about the last days of Philip Seymour Hoffman, the actor who died last week at 46 of an apparent heroin overdose. Yet Mr. Hoffman's case, despite its uncertainties, high-lights some new truths about addiction and several long-known risks for overdose.

The actor, who quit heroin more than 20 years ago, reportedly struggled to break a prescription painkiller habit last year. Experts in addiction say that the use of medications like Vicodin, OxyContin and oxycodone — all opiates like heroin — has altered the landscape of addiction and relapse, in ways that affect both current users and former ones.

"The old-school user, pre-1990s, mostly used just heroin, and if there was none around, went through withdrawal," said Stephen E. Lankenau, a sociologist at Drexel University who has surveyed young addicts. Today, he said, "users switch back and forth, to pills then back to heroin when it's available, and back again. The two have become integrated."

Rates of prescription opiate abuse have risen steadily over the last decade, while the number of people reporting that they used heroin in the past 12 months has nearly doubled since 2007 to 620,000, according to government statistics. That's no coincidence, researchers argue: more people than ever now get a taste of opiates at a young age, and recovering addicts live in a world with far more temptations than there were a generation ago.

"You can get the pills from so many sources," said Traci Rieckmann, an addiction researcher at Oregon Health & Science University. "There's no paraphernalia, no smell. It's the perfect drug, for many people."

Millions of people use these drugs safely, and doctors generally prescribe them conscientiously. But for some patients, prescription painkillers can act as an introduction — or a reintroduction — to an opiate high. The pills set off heroin craving in recovering addicts, doctors say, every bit as well as they soothe withdrawal in current users.

Dr. Jason Jerry, an addiction specialist at the Cleveland Clinic's Alcohol and Drug Recovery Center, estimates that half of the 200 or so heroin addicts the clinic sees every month started on prescription opiates.

"Often it's a legitimate prescription, but next thing they know, they're obtaining the pills illicitly," Dr. Jerry said.

Kaylee, 19, left, exchanged used needles for clean ones at a clinic in Portland, Me.

In many parts of the country, heroin is much cheaper than prescription opiates. "So people eventually say, 'Why am I paying $1 per milligram for oxy when for a tenth of the price I can get an equivalent dose of heroin?' " Dr. Jerry said.

Investigators do not yet know whether Mr. Hoffman was taking prescription opiates at the time of his death. Toxicology tests are pending, and the purity and content of the heroin found in his apartment will certainly be a focus.

While the deluge of prescription painkillers is new, other risk factors for overdose have not changed in decades.

Post-rehab — after having gotten clean — addicts are vulnerable to overdose because they misjudge their tolerance level, which has dropped. Pre-rehab, many addicts will binge one last time, also inviting trouble.

"These are common danger zones," said Dr. Nicholas L. Gideonse, the medical director of O.H.S.U. Richmond Community Health Center in Portland.

Even a change in where a person uses his or her drug of choice can increase the likelihood of an overdose, studies suggest. "If you habitually use in your car, for example, the body prepares itself to receive the drug when it's in that environment," Dr. Rieckmann said. "It's called conditioned tolerance. When people using are in an unfamiliar places, the body is less physically prepared."

The risk of dying from an overdose is higher when people are using alone. "Another person, sober or not, can notice when someone nods off, or just say, 'Hey man, slow down,' " Dr. Lankenau said. "And users act as a gauge for each other of when they're doing something dangerous."

Many needle exchange programs and clinics now have overdose prevention courses, teaching users to notice danger signs and administer the drug naloxone, an opiate blocker that E.M.T.s use to revive addicts who have overdosed.

None of which might have spared Mr. Hoffman. One thing that has not changed for heroin addicts over the past 20 years is the certainty that this next shot will not be deadly.

"You have to understand that addicts inject three or four times a day for years and years on end," Dr. Gideonse said. "They don't perceive any one shot to be dangerous or potentially deadly, because in their experience, there's no reason to."

Heroin Scourge Overtakes a 'Quaint' Vermont Town

BY KATHARINE Q. SEELYE | MARCH 5, 2014

BENNINGTON, VT. — Stephanie Predel, a stick-thin 23-year-old freshly out of jail, said she was off heroin. But she knows precisely where she could get more drugs if she ever wanted them — at the support meetings for addicts.

"I can get most of my drugs right at the meeting," she said. "Drug dealers go because they know they're going to get business." She added, "People are going into the bathroom to get high."

Bennington, a pre-Revolutionary town of 17,000 people, presents another face of the heroin epidemic that has swept through Vermont.

In January, Gov. Peter Shumlin devoted his entire State of the State address to what he said was a "full-blown heroin crisis" gripping the state. In an interview later, he said that the state's localities had managed only a patchwork response. Citing Rutland's antidrug crusade as a hopeful sign, he said that not all areas had felt the same urgency.

"Bennington is where Rutland was four years ago," he said.

Known for its pottery and its classical music, Bennington exudes an early American gentility. A distinctive bell tower sits atop the Old First Congregational Church, where Robert Frost is buried. An obelisk commemorates victory over the British at the Battle of Bennington (1777).

But the 21st-century drug scourge is evident in the faces of some of the young people hanging out near the Stewart's convenience store on Main Street.

"The quaint town of Bennington has had a rude awakening of drugs," said Wayne Godfrey, a Vermont state trooper, as he cruised the streets here one recent frigid morning. "Everyone is doing it," he said of heroin. "It's in the high school. The kids are doing it right in school. You find Baggies in the hallway."

Stephanie Predel is off heroin. But the Bennington, Vt., area, where she lives, is in the throes of an epidemic.

Two sting operations, one of them believed to be the biggest drug sweep in Vermont history, took place here last year. But Officer James A. Gulley Jr. of the Bennington Police Department said that arrests had not stanched the drug flow. "You send one person to jail," he said, "and everyone else says, 'I'm going in and taking over that market.' "

People in Bennington trying to wean themselves from opioids have access to substitutes like buprenorphine and to counseling, but the nearest methadone clinic is an hour away.

That is a hardship for Lloyd Wright, who is 42 but looks much older and lives in a motel room on the outskirts of town with his two dogs and two cats. He said he stopped using heroin recently but his craving persists. He has been so desperate, he said, that he had a dentist pull out his top teeth on one side, hoping he could get a batch of painkillers. "I had a few bad teeth, but I had all of them pulled because I figured I'd get more pills," he said, opening his mouth wide to reveal his toothless gums. He got the pills, but went through them in one day.

Alfred Hickey, 42, said he quit heroin cold turkey recently after being on a waiting list for a treatment program and not getting in. "I use mind over matter," he said. "If I don't mind, it doesn't matter."

Dr. Trey Dobson, chief medical officer at Southwestern Vermont Medical Center, said that since Governor Shumlin's speech, a coalition of health care providers and others had begun discussing what services, including methadone and Suboxone, would best meet Bennington's needs. Methadone requires tighter protocols and a more elaborate medical infrastructure than other maintenance drugs.

And such clinics are not always welcome. "A lot of people are afraid that if you build it, they will come, and they don't want a bunch of addicts hanging around," said Paul Doucette, Bennington's police chief. "I hate to say it, but guess what? We already have them."

Vermont ranks high on Gallup's "well-being" index, but several recovering addicts here say they do not feel a part of that Vermont. They do not ski, or have jobs, or have much to look forward to.

Hailey Clark, 20, is just out of jail, where she was forced to quit her heroin habit. With a felony conviction for selling and possession, she cannot find work. She has no home and is staying with a friend. Just above one of her puffy white boots is a thick piece of GPS hardware, which monitors her every move. She aches for her young son, who is in her mother's custody, but knows she is in no position to care for him. "I'm not ready yet to get him back," she said, wiping a tear with the cuff of her sweater. "I don't have anything for him, and I don't want to rip him out of my mom's house and bring him to nothing."

Adding to their hopelessness is the seemingly endless New England winter.

"There's nothing to do here," said Ms. Predel, whose addiction also cost her custody of her three children and who is now staying with her mother in Bennington County in a former hunting cabin. "Come wintertime, everyone is inside using."

New York Is a Hub in a Surging Heroin Trade

BY J. DAVID GOODMAN | MAY 19, 2014

THE FLOOD OF HEROIN coming into and going out of New York City has surged to the highest levels in more than two decades, alarming law enforcement officials who say that bigger players are now entering the market to sell the drug here and to feed a growing appetite along the East Coast.

The amount of heroin seized in investigations involving the city's special narcotics prosecutor has already surpassed last year's totals, and is higher than any year going back to 1991.

The drug makes its way here in trucks rumbling north from Mexico; as they get closer to New York, they park at truck stops or warehouses to transfer loads of heroin to cars bound for mills in the Bronx or Upper Manhattan and, eventually, to users along the Eastern Seaboard at prices ranging from $6 to $10 per glassine envelope.

The rise in heroin use nationwide has been well documented, as the drug has created addicts and caused the deaths of well-known figures, like the actor Philip Seymour Hoffman, and young people in middle-class families from Staten Island to Vermont.

What the authorities are seeing now is the outgrowth of all that drug abuse, said Bridget G. Brennan, the special narcotics prosecutor whose office deals primarily with large-scale operations: far-flung drug organizations accelerating to meet heroin demand by setting up New York operations that are growing in sophistication and output.

"We're kind of the head of the Hydra," said Ms. Brennan, who is scheduled to testify about heroin trends during a City Council budget hearing on Tuesday. "This is highly organized, high volume, and it's being moved much more efficiently and effectively to reach out to a broader user base."

Her office recorded more than 288 pounds of heroin seized in the first four months of 2014, a figure that does not account for the everyday, street-level drug deals in the city. On Staten Island, where dealers are often users themselves and the rate of overdose is the city's highest, the office has no heroin cases because there are few big-time players there, authorities said.

Nonetheless, in arrests of users and dealers, Staten Island narcotics detectives have recorded a steep increase in the amount of heroin taken off the street there so far this year — up 61 percent compared with 2013. Detectives are also beginning to find organized networks of dealers there, in what had long been a haven of low crime rates and unlocked doors.

"It's cheap, it's potent and there's a user demand here right now and they're flooding the market," said James J. Hunt, who heads the Drug Enforcement Administration's New York office. "In my time, we've never seen the amount of large heroin seizures like this."

Roughly 35 percent of heroin seized by the Drug Enforcement Administration nationwide since October was confiscated by agents in New York State. In years past, the state has accounted for about one-fifth of heroin seizures nationwide.

Mr. Hunt said that distributors of drugs favor locating hubs in New York City for the same reason that business have flocked here for centuries: a big local market and easy access to other East Coast areas.

Nearly all of the heroin feeding the city passes through the Bronx and Upper Manhattan, where it is divided up into glassine bags in so-called heroin mills, stamped with a brand and bundled for distribution and sale. One recent raid, in March, turned up a piece of paper listing possible brand names, as well as those already used, and stamped bags with an image of Heisenberg, a character from the TV show "Breaking Bad."

The latest example came Monday, as the authorities announced the arrest of two suspected high-level traffickers in one Bronx-based drug organization, and seizure of 53 pounds of heroin along with assault rifles, $85,000 in cash and about 20 pounds of cocaine. Federal agents and officers tracked the two suspects' drug-laden cars across state lines to a low-rise apartment building in Hartford, officials said, rushing in before the drugs could be poured down the sink.

For users in the city, that proximity to the distribution points means lower prices than in other areas of the country. Mr. Hunt said a kilogram of heroin could go for as little as $40,000 in New York City but as much as $80,000 in Springfield, Mass. "Every pair of hands it goes through, you're taking on money," he said.

Ms. Brennan said that in many of her cases, the Sinaloa cartel, Mexico's largest, is exporting the heroin using familiar cocaine trafficking routes and arranging to have the drug transported in otherwise legitimate tractor-trailer trucks. The ability of the cartel — known for distributing cocaine and marijuana — to capitalize on a lucrative market for heroin does not appear to have been dampened by the February arrest of its leader, Joaquín Guzmán Loera, known as El Chapo. Other organizations have also joined in, Mr. Hunt said.

Across New York City, the Police Department logged seizures of 786 pounds of heroin in 2013, the highest such number in at least five years. So far this year, officers have seized 217 pounds of heroin, versus 139 pounds last year at this time, according to department statistics.

The arrest of the two suspected Bronx-based traffickers announced on Monday provided a small glimpse into a typical heroin distribution center.

The suspects, Guillermo Esteban Margarin, 33, and Edualin Tapia, 28, carried the drug from a seventh-floor Bronx apartment near Interstate 87 in suitcases and a white box, the authorities said. The men drove the drugs up to a Hartford safe house, one in a Jeep Cherokee and the other in an Acura sedan, the authorities said. They were arrested there on Friday.

A search the next day of a storage unit off Interstate 95 in the Bronx turned up a pair of assault rifles, a handgun and kilogram presses, which are used to create packages of drugs that mimic the look of uncut heroin just delivered from across the border, Ms. Brennan said.

Both men were charged with felony drug possession and conspiracy; they are awaiting extradition from Hartford to New York.

Drug Linked to Ohio Overdoses Can Kill in Doses Smaller than a Snowflake

BY JACK HEALY | SEPT. 5, 2016

CINCINNATI — On the day he almost died, John Hatmaker bought a packet of Oreos and some ruby-red Swedish Fish at the corner store for his 5-year-old son. He was walking home when he spotted a man who used to sell him heroin.

Mr. Hatmaker, 29, had overdosed seven times in the four years he had been addicted to pain pills and heroin. But he hoped he was past all that. He had planned to spend that Saturday afternoon, Aug. 27, showing his son the motorcycles and enjoying the music at a prayer rally for Hope Over Heroin in this region stricken by soaring rates of drug overdoses and opioid deaths.

But first, he decided as he palmed a sample folded into a square of paper, he would snort this.

As he crumpled to the sidewalk, Mr. Hatmaker became one of more than 200 people to overdose in the Cincinnati area in the past two weeks, leaving three people dead in what the officials here called an unprecedented spike. Similar increases in overdoses have rippled recently through Indiana, Kentucky and West Virginia, overwhelming ambulance crews and emergency rooms and stunning some anti-drug advocates.

Addiction specialists said the sharp increases in overdoses were a grim symptom of America's heroin epidemic, and of the growing prevalence of powerful synthetic opiates like fentanyl. The synthetics are often mixed into batches of heroin, or sprinkled into mixtures of caffeine, antihistamines and other fillers.

In Cincinnati, some medical and law enforcement officials said they believed the overdoses were largely caused by a synthetic drug

Syringes scattered along the ground at a homeless encampment in Lawrence, Mass.

called carfentanil, an animal tranquilizer used on livestock and elephants with no practical uses for humans. Fentanyl can be 50 times stronger than heroin, and carfentanil is as much as 100 times more potent than fentanyl. Experts said an amount smaller than a snowflake could kill a person.

Dr. Lakshmi Kode Sammarco, the coroner here in Hamilton County, said her office had determined that carfentanil was the cause of several recent overdose deaths, the first confirmed cases in the county. Investigators are now examining deaths back to early July to see if carfentanil was the cause.

"We'd never seen it before," Dr. Sammarco said in an interview, while toxicologists and drug specialists on the third floor of the coroner's office tested blood samples and small bags of white powder. "I'm really worried about this."

Officials suspect the carfentanil is being manufactured in China or Mexico and is making its way to the Cincinnati area in heroin shipments that flow north on Interstates 71 and 75. The drug has shown up in Columbus, Ohio, the Gulf Coast of Florida and central Kentucky, according to local news reports.

Fentanyl is widely used in hospitals as a fast-acting painkiller, but Dr. Sammarco said carfentanil is rare. She said she had to call zoos, rural veterinarians, federal law enforcement authorities and a licensed manufacturer in Canada to find a sample that her office could use to calibrate their drug-testing equipment.

Around Cincinnati, police officers and sheriff's deputies are so concerned about the potency of carfentanil and other synthetic opioids that they carry overdose-reversing naloxone sprays for themselves, in case they accidentally inhale or touch the tiniest flake.

Because of its potency, law enforcement agents have stopped field-testing the powders they find at the scenes of overdoses. When regional drug enforcement officers in Cincinnati pulled over two men on Aug. 26 and found an unknown pink substance, they sent it directly to the county coroner's office; it tested positive for heroin, fentanyl and carfentanil.

And as ambulance crews and the police rushed to respond to this recent wave of overdoses, answering 20 or 30 calls each day, they said they sometimes had to give people two, three or five doses of naloxone spray to revive them. Usually, one quick spray is enough to block a person's opiate receptors and immediately jolt them out of an overdose. Some hospitals have had to give overdose patients intravenous drips of anti-opioid chemicals.

"Our antidote, our Narcan, is ineffective," Sheriff Jim Neil of Hamilton County said, using a trade name for naloxone. "It was meant for heroin. It wasn't meant for fentanyl or carfentanil."

Like much of the country, officials here along the Ohio-Kentucky border have been straining to cope with the toll of opioid use.

Accidental drug overdose deaths in Hamilton County doubled to 414 last year from 204 in 2012, according to the county coroner, most of those involving fentanyl or heroin.

There were an average of 92 overdose reports each month during the first six months of 2016, up from an average of 40 during the last half of 2015, according to numbers collected by the Greater Cincinnati Fusion Center, a regional law enforcement and public health group.

As deaths mounted, officials formed anti-heroin coalitions and task forces. Police officers and addiction experts visited the homes of people who had overdosed to try to persuade them into treatment. The Cincinnati Enquirer even has a heroin beat reporter.

Nan Franks, the executive director of the Addiction Services Council, the Cincinnati affiliate of the National Council on Alcoholism and Drug Dependence, said the problem was made worse by scarce bed space at the area's lone publicly funded detox center and a constant lack of money for treatment services.

Ms. Franks said drugs were so cheap that addicts said they can walk through one housing project and get four free samples from dealers.

"People are waiting for treatment," Ms. Franks said. "We need a better response to keep them safe."

Five days after Mr. Hatmaker overdosed, a police car pulled up outside his home in Norwood, an independent city of 20,000 inside Cincinnati. Lt. Tom Fallon, the commander of the county's heroin task force, was there to take Mr. Hatmaker to treatment.

As they drove, Mr. Hatmaker thought back to how he had gotten there. He said he started selling pain pills in 2012 after being laid off from his job at an online retailer's warehouse, then started taking them, then turned to heroin. Cycles of withdrawal, jail and treatment followed. Some of his friends died or went to prison for selling drugs.

He said he does not remember much from this latest overdose — only waking in an ambulance and feeling the pain where medics had pounded his chest to keep him alive. The medics who saved him told him he was minutes from death, Mr. Hatmaker said.

"I'm tired of this," he said. "I'm tired of overdosing; I'm tired of this life. Eventually, you're just going to die."

The First Count of Fentanyl Deaths in 2016: Up 540% in Three Years

BY JOSH KATZ | SEPT. 2, 2017

DRUG OVERDOSES killed roughly 64,000 people in the United States last year, according to the first governmental account of nationwide drug deaths to cover all of 2016. It's a staggering rise of more than 22 percent over the 52,404 drug deaths recorded the previous year — and even higher than The New York Times's estimate in June, which was based on earlier preliminary data.

Drug overdoses are expected to remain the leading cause of death for Americans under 50, as synthetic opioids — primarily fentanyl and its analogues — continue to push the death count higher. Drug deaths involving fentanyl more than doubled from 2015 to 2016, accompanied by an upturn in deaths involving cocaine and methamphetamines. Together they add up to an epidemic of drug overdoses that is killing people at a faster rate than the H.I.V. epidemic at its peak.

This is the first national data to break down the growth by drug and by state. We've known for a while that fentanyls were behind the growing count of drug deaths in some states and counties. But now we can see the extent to which this is true nationally, as deaths involving synthetic opioids, mostly fentanyls, have risen to more than 20,000 from 3,000 in just three years.

Deaths involving prescription opioids continue to rise, but many of those deaths also involved heroin, fentanyl or a fentanyl analogue. There is a downward trend in deaths from prescription opioids alone. At the same time, there has been a resurgence in cocaine and methamphetamine deaths. Many of these also involve opioids, but a significant portion of drug deaths — roughly one-third in 2015 — do not.

About 300 grams of fentanyl have been confiscated in Haverhill, Mass., within the past month.

The explosion in fentanyl deaths and the persistence of widespread opioid addiction have swamped local and state resources. Communities say their budgets are being strained by the additional needs — for increased police and medical care, for widespread naloxone distribution and for a stronger foster care system that can handle the swelling number of neglected or orphaned children.

It's an epidemic hitting different parts of the country in different ways. People are accustomed to thinking of the opioid crisis as a rural white problem, with accounts of Appalachian despair and the plight of New England heroin addicts. But fentanyls are changing the equation: The death rate in Maryland last year outpaced that in both Kentucky and Maine.

This provisional data, compiled by the National Center for Health Statistics, was produced in response to requests from government officials after reporting from The Times in June. An early version of the report was posted online last month and will be formally published by the N.C.H.S. in the coming weeks. According to Robert Anderson, the agency's chief of mortality statistics, the document is the first edition of what will be a monthly report on the latest provisional overdose death counts.

Because of delays in drug death reporting, the data is mostly but not entirely complete. The final numbers, released in December, could be even higher.

It's too early to know what 2017 will hold, but anecdotal reports from state health departments and county coroners and medical examiners suggest that the overdose epidemic has continued to worsen. In March, President Trump created a commission to study the crisis. The commission's interim report made a number of recommendations, but the administration has yet to take concrete action on any of them.

Despite Trump's Pleas, China's Online Opioid Bazaar Is Booming

BY SUI-LEE WEE AND JAVIER C. HERNÁNDEZ | NOV. 8, 2017

SHANGHAI — President Trump is looking to President Xi Jinping to "do something" about America's opioid epidemic, for which he blames China.

That won't be easy.

Buying opioids from China, despite legal prohibitions, remains as easy as providing money and a shipping address. A drug bazaar thrives on Chinese websites, providing one-stop shopping for users around the world.

On Weiku.com, a website based in the eastern city of Hangzhou, close to 100 Chinese companies say they sell fentanyl, a powerful synthetic opioid. Vendors on one Beijing-based website, Mfrbee.com, sell chicken nuggets, basketball jerseys and carfentanil, the elephant tranquilizer that is 10,000 times as potent as morphine. A Shanghai-based chemical company, Shanghai Kaiwodun Biochemical, says it offers the designer drug U-47700 for $1,450 a pound.

A Kaiwodun sales agent said over a Skype text message that the company had many customers in the United States and time-tested methods for shipping, sending photos of brown sugar and monosodium glutamate packets and a fuel filter.

Weiku removed the search results for fentanyl on its website after The New York Times called the company for comment. A Weiku representative, Liu Congjuan, said that the company banned the advertising of fentanyl on its website but that sellers circumvented the prohibition by making slight tweaks to the forbidden search term.

A representative for Mfrbee.com said the company was unaware of the listing and would delete it if it was illegal. Kaiwodun did not immediately respond to questions sent via email and Skype text.

Mr. Trump has accused China of being the main source of the "flood of cheap and deadly fentanyl" into America. In a news conference last week, Wei Xiaojun, a senior Chinese official, disputed Mr. Trump's assertion, saying there was no evidence for it.

On Thursday, in an appearance in Beijing with Mr. Xi, Mr. Trump said he brought up the issue of fentanyl with his Chinese counterpart. "We're going to be focusing on it very strongly, the president and myself," Mr. Trump said.

Fentanyl is a synthetic painkiller that is 30 to 50 times as powerful as heroin. It is becoming more popular among users because of its potency — it takes less than a milligram for a single use — and relatively cheap cost. Drug investigators say a worrying trend is the mixing of fentanyl with heroin or oxycodone, another popular painkiller, or counterfeit prescription pills — all sold to unwitting users.

The ease of buying opioids from China illustrates how difficult it will be for the United States to win the war on the worst drug epidemic in American history. While China has pledged to work with the United States to stop the flow of opioids, experts say it will be tough because of the country's lax regulation of chemical companies, a sprawling industry of more than 30,000 businesses that face few requirements for transparency.

"The challenge is that when the chemical industry is so big like it is in China, policing it is incredibly difficult," said Jeremy Douglas, the regional representative of the United Nations Office on Drugs and Crime for Southeast Asia and the Pacific.

"Regulating it — I wouldn't say it's impossible — but it is no small task."

Analysts say Chinese chemical makers have exploited weak regulation to make the nation the world's top producer of fentanyl. Mr. Trump has said fentanyl from China is "either shipped into the United States or smuggled across the southern border by drug traffickers." The Drug Enforcement Administration said stopping the flow was a top priority.

Kai Pflug, a management consultant in the Chinese chemical industry, said that producers of fentanyl were able to avoid detection in part because they labeled their products as industrial rather than pharmaceutical, subjecting them to less stringent regulation.

"As long as, in China, you can produce chemicals without serious supervision," Mr. Pflug said, "the problem will persist."

Chinese regulators say they struggle with the speed at which chemists are able to produce new variations on fentanyl, circumventing the government's ban on 23 fentanyl analogues.

China takes a hard-line stance on drugs domestically, executing drug traffickers and policing consumption. History textbooks and television shows widely depict how the country was ravaged by opium addiction in the 19th century, a major driver in the Opium Wars.

According to the Brookings Institution, Chinese users' drugs of choice are ketamine, an anesthetic, or methamphetamine, a stimulant. Despite the lack of a domestic fentanyl abuse problem, Beijing said its list of banned fentanyl analogues was longer than that of the United Nations' antidrug agency. Officials say this is a sign of the government's willingness to assist the United States.

Beijing has not always been so helpful. Jorge Guajardo, a former Mexican ambassador to China, said he and other top Mexican officials repeatedly lobbied Chinese officials to stop the export of fentanyl precursors to Mexico.

"They always said: 'It's a problem for Mexico to deal with. It's a problem with your customs. There's nothing we can do,' " said Mr. Guajardo, who was ambassador from 2007 to 2013. "When the U.S. takes it up, it very quickly becomes their problem, because the U.S. has many other ways of retaliating."

Mr. Trump has declared the opioid crisis a public health emergency after drug overdoses — mostly caused by fentanyl and its analogues — resulted in more than 64,000 deaths, including that of the music star Prince, in the United States last year.

Mr. Douglas of the United Nations said the Chinese authorities were moving quickly to cooperate. "They are working closely with us; they are working with the U.S. and Canada," he said. "Obviously there is frustration because there's a lot of political pressure in the U.S. and Canada right now to take action on this."

In a sign that the United States was taking its fight against opioids globally, the Department of Justice last month announced indictments against two Chinese men it accused of being major fentanyl traffickers. The department said the men were responsible for the deaths of several opioid users in America.

At last week's news conference, Mr. Wei, of the Ministry of Public Security, criticized the public announcement, saying it would hinder the case that both Beijing and Washington were working on. When asked whether China would help the United States in the extradition of the men, Mr. Wei was noncommittal, saying it depended in part on the evidence it received from America, which has no extradition treaty with China.

In China, fentanyl makers are constantly finding new ways to evade detection. A sales agent from Shanghai Changhong Chemical Technology asked for payment by Bitcoin or a money transfer that allows the recipient to be anonymous. A sales representative from Cinri Biological Technology, a company based in the central city of Wuhan, promised to conceal the fentanyl in cat food packets — and to resend any seized deliveries.

One Changhong agent acknowledged a Chinese ban on shipping U-47700 and other products but said it could still deliver via EMS, China's state-owned express mail provider. EMS did not immediately respond to a request for comment.

Both Cinri and Changhong declined to provide phone numbers. When asked for comment, the Cinri representative responded over Skype text with the Russian word for imbecile and went silent. The Changhong representative did not respond to a request for comment.

Many Chinese chemical companies scoff at Mr. Trump's calls for greater regulation, saying that they already face onerous demands from the Chinese government and that they are only serving customers.

Producers of fentanyl in China say they manufacture the chemical for legitimate purposes such as making painkillers for cancer patients.

"What role do we have in creating this problem?" said Cindy Wang, a saleswoman for a chemical company in Wuhan, which has sold fentanyl legitimately in the past. She spoke on condition that her firm not be identified. "It is up to the American people to deal with this issue."

Fentanyl Adds Deadly Kick to Opioid Woes in Britain

BY CEYLAN YEGINSU | FEB. 4, 2018

KINGSTON UPON HULL, ENGLAND — There was something different in the batches of heroin that circulated through this English port city over the summer, but most addicts had no idea what it was until their friends and fellow addicts, 16 in all, had died of overdoses.

Those who tried the drug described a "warm," "euphoric" high, followed by a sudden knockout effect, one that has killed dozens of Britons over the past year and left hundreds hospitalized.

The new kick came from fentanyl, an opiate painkiller 50 to 100 times more powerful than morphine, that was mixed in with the heroin. The drug has killed thousands of Americans, including the rock stars Prince and Tom Petty, but the lethal risk it poses has barely deterred addicts in Kingston Upon Hull, known familiarly as Hull. In fact, many of them cannot get enough of it.

"It makes all the pain go away," said Chris, 32, a homeless resident of Hull who has been addicted to heroin for more than eight years.

Britain already has Europe's highest proportion of heroin addicts, and last year, drug-related deaths hit a record high in England and Wales, with 3,744 deaths mainly from heroin and other opioids. While the scale is small compared with deaths in the United States — where more than 100 Americans die each day from opioid abuse — British authorities fear that fentanyl could become the country's next most dangerous drug.

"People here are prescribed opioids for pain, but nothing to the extent of the U.S., where extremely potent opioids are being prescribed on a large scale," said Dr. Prun Bijral, the medical director for Change, Grow, Live, a nonprofit organization that focuses on substance abuse. "On the one hand, this is positive. But on the other hand, the U.K. has one of the highest rates of drug-related deaths in Europe."

A mural commemorating the fishing industry in Kingston Upon Hull, England. Since the collapse of the fishing industry in the 1970s, the city has some of the highest unemployment and addiction rates in the country.

No place has been hit harder by heroin, fentanyl and opioid addiction recently than Hull, a former fishing town of 260,000 people about 150 miles north of London that was improbably named Britain's 2017 "City of Culture." On a drizzly cold day last month, under a bright green sign welcoming visitors to the city, several addicts lay bundled up, stashes of drugs and alcohol secreted in blankets and other belongings. Others lined the doorways of nondescript buildings on the city's main street.

Since the fishing industry collapsed in the 1970s, the city has suffered some of the highest rates of unemployment — currently 8.9 percent — and addiction in the country. The city's easy transport links to the port and two major highways also facilitate drug trafficking.

In recent years, the city has started to bounce back with a series of investments, including a $400 million wind turbine facility and a

$30 million research center that aims to develop new treatments for drug addicts.

But Hull continues to catch the most national attention for issues relating to drug abuse. And lately, those miseries have been compounded by fentanyl, which has been blamed for at least 60 deaths nationwide, the National Crime Agency said, and has emerged as a favorite of addicts like Chris.

On this gloomy day, he was lying in the doorway of a derelict building slumped over a plastic bag of his belongings, his hands furiously shaking.

Chris, who declined to provide his last name because he did not want his family to read about his addiction, said he first tried heroin when he was rejected for a job after two years in unemployment.

"I got so hammered that I took my anger out on my girlfriend," he said. "I smashed her head in the wall and just left her and went and bought heroin. I've been using ever since."

When he first experienced fentanyl last year, he did not know what he had taken. "I took a shot and it felt like I exploded. It's dynamite kind of strong," he said, inadvertently describing why drug experts consider the drug so dangerous.

Several people in Hull who said they had collapsed after trying fentanyl vowed never to take it again. But there are still many like Chris who actively seek it out, even after a recent police crackdown slowed the supply coming into Hull.

Even though the police acknowledge the scope and severity of the problem, it was relatively easy, and inexpensive, for an addict to buy the drug, as an afternoon spent with Chris showed.

He spoke openly about his addiction, and explained that all the money he earned from begging — an average of $40 a day — was spent on drugs and alcohol. He receives free food at the local soup kitchen or through donations.

Out on the street, he occasionally stopped to ask people for money, but he had enough in his pocket to pick up his next stash, which he said cost 12 pounds, around $16.

PHIL HATCHER-MOORE FOR THE NEW YORK TIMES

A man identified only as Lee, 42, who used to do heroin every day, says he has been clean since moving into a squat opened by activists. He has been on the streets since June, and said he had friends who died after using fentanyl.

After picking up the drug from his dealer, he went to the house of a friend, Billy Kenwood, who was also an addict but had stopped taking fentanyl after he nearly died from an overdose last year. As he recounted the incident, Chris busied himself preparing to shoot up — strapping his arm to find a vein, heating up the heroin mixed with fentanyl and finally injecting the liquid.

"There we go, bliss," he said, before gradually starting to slump down in his chair.

"Some people go out like that after taking fenny and don't wake up," Mr. Kenwood said.

One homeless couple who sleep in the city center said they had lost at least six friends to fentanyl overdoses over the past year. They had both tried the drug, and like most other addicts and former users interviewed for this article, said they liked it.

But they also overdosed.

"I woke up in an ambulance and they told me I had taken fentanyl. They said if they got to me 2 to 3 minutes later, I would have died," said Mark Stevenson, 45.

The couple say they have been clean from heroin and fentanyl for several months now, but many of their friends are addicted and have been suffering from severe withdrawal symptoms as supplies of fentanyl have grown scarcer in the recent crackdown.

"My friend was shooting four to five times more heroin to try and get the same effect as fentanyl," Mr. Stevenson said.

Some drug gangs have reportedly started to make fentanyl in home labs to keep up with the demand. Britain accounts for the largest number of fentanyl sales on the limited access darknet in Europe, with 1,000 trades being made in recent months, research by the Oxford Internet institute found.

"There is money to be made. For a very small amount of drug you can get a lot of doses and lots of potential individual sales," Dr. Bijral said.

An even more lethal opioid known as carfentanil, an elephant tranquilizer 100 times stronger than fentanyl, has been cited in several recent fatal overdoses in Hull. Local people say the police carried out several operations in recent months in an effort to cut off the supply. But a former drug addict who lives in the area says that if people are seeking it, they can still find it.

In recent weeks, Hull's local council boarded up a canopy that had provided shelter for several addicts in the city center, but said in a statement that support and accommodation options had been provided for the homeless people who had camped there.

Some of them have chosen to stay in hostels, while others are squatting in a derelict building with help from volunteers. But both facilities have zero tolerance for drugs and alcohol, and that has caused some to move away.

Chris has since left Hull and has not been seen in the city for over a month. "The fenny has dried up," Mr. Kenwood said. "He's gone up north to find some."

Meth, the Forgotten Killer, Is Back. And It's Everywhere.

BY FRANCES ROBLES | FEB. 13, 2018

PORTLAND, ORE. — They huddled against the biting wind, pacing from one corner to another hoping to score heroin or pills. But a different drug was far more likely to be on offer outside the train station downtown, where homeless drug users live in tents pitched on the sidewalk.

"Everybody has meth around here — everybody," said Sean, a 27-year-old heroin user who hangs out downtown and gave only his first name. "It's the easiest to find."

The scourge of crystal meth, with its exploding labs and ruinous effect on teeth and skin, has been all but forgotten amid national concern over the opioid crisis. But 12 years after Congress took aggressive action to curtail it, meth has returned with a vengeance. Here in Oregon, meth-related deaths vastly outnumber those from heroin. At the United States border, agents are seizing 10 to 20 times the amounts they did a decade ago. Methamphetamine, experts say, has never been purer, cheaper or more lethal.

Oregon took a hard line against meth in 2006, when it began requiring a doctor's prescription to buy the nasal decongestant used to make it. "It was like someone turned off a switch," said J.R. Ujifusa, a senior prosecutor in Multnomah County, which includes Portland.

"But where there is a void," he added, "someone fills it."

The decades-long effort to fight methamphetamine is a tale with two takeaways. One: The number of domestic meth labs has declined precipitously, and along with it the number of children harmed and police officers sickened by exposure to dangerous chemicals. But also, two: There is more meth on the streets today, more people are using it, and more of them are dying.

Drugs go through cycles — in the 1980s and early '90s, the use of crack cocaine surged. In the early 2000s, meth made from pseudoephedrine,

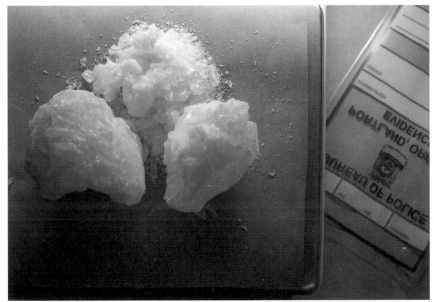

Methamphetamine, confiscated by the Portland Police Bureau in Portalnd, Ore. The drug, experts say, has never been purer cheaper, or more lethal.

the decongestant in drugstore products like Sudafed, poured out of domestic labs like those in the early seasons of the hit television show "Breaking Bad."

Narcotics squads became glorified hazmat teams, spending entire shifts on cleanup. In 2004, the Portland police responded to 114 meth houses. "We rolled from meth lab to meth lab," said Sgt. Jan M. Kubic of the county sheriff's office. "Patrol would roll up on a domestic violence call, and there'd be a lab in the kitchen. Everything would come to a screeching halt."

In 2005 Congress passed the Combat Methamphetamine Act, which put pseudoephedrine behind the counter, limited sales to 7.5 grams per customer in a 30-day period and required pharmacies to track sales. Although some meth makers tried "smurfing," sending emissaries to several stores to make purchases, meth cases plummeted.

States like Oregon and Mississippi required a prescription, making smurfing almost impossible. And a new epidemic took hold: prescription painkillers and opiates like heroin. With no more meth lab explosions on the nightly news, the public forgot about the drug.

But meth, it turns out, was only on hiatus. When the ingredients became difficult to come by in the United States, Mexican drug cartels stepped in. Now fighting meth often means seizing large quantities of ready-made product in highway stops.

The cartels have inundated the market with so much pure, low-cost meth that dealers have more of it than they know what to do with. Under pressure from traffickers to unload large quantities, law enforcement officials say, dealers are even offering meth to customers on credit. In Portland, the drug has made inroads in black neighborhoods, something experienced narcotics investigators say was unheard of five years ago.

"I have been involved with meth for the last 25 years. A wholesale plummet of price per pound, combined with a huge increase in purity, tells me they have perfected the production or manufacturing of methamphetamine," said Steven Bell, a spokesman for the Drug Enforcement Administration. "They have figured out the chemical reactions to get the best bang for their bucks."

Nearly 100 percent pure and about $5 a hit, the new meth is all the more difficult to resist. "We're seeing a lot of longtime addicts who used crack cocaine switch to meth," said Brandon Combs, a Portland officer assigned to the street crimes unit. "You ask them about it, and they'll say: 'Hey, it's half the price, and it's good quality.' "

Nationally, nearly 6,000 people died from stimulant use — mostly meth — in 2015, a 255 increase from 2005, according to the Centers for Disease Control and Prevention. The percentage of the nation's drug overdose toll that was attributed to stimulants inched up to 11 percent of the deaths.

United States Customs and Border Protection statistics show that in the last five years, the amount of meth seized has tripled, while the

A person injects a combination of methamphetamine and heroin in Portland. Meth arrests in Oregon rose 64 percent from 2011 to 2015, the only drug-related arrest category to increase.

seizures for other drugs have declined or had only modest increases.

In Oregon, 232 people died from meth use in 2016, nearly twice as many as died from heroin — and three times as many as died from meth 10 years before, according to the state Department of Health.

Between 2011 and 2015, meth arrests were the only type of drug arrests in Portland to increase, and meth has the highest correlation with serious crimes. More than one in five burglars and nearly 40 percent of car thieves were also charged with meth crimes, according to the Portland Police Bureau.

"Heroin is a depressant. It shuts you down and you're not capable of doing a whole lot," Sergeant Kubic said. Meth is a stimulant: "Tweakers are jacked up. They have lowered inhibitions and are awake 24/7, running around at night, so burglaries become easier."

Eric, a former dancer in Portland, who asked that his last name not be published, said he now worked as a "professional booster." Pawnshop owners give him "laundry lists" of coveted items, and he goes out and steals them, getting 50 cents on the dollar.

The cartels' efficiency has flooded the market far beyond Oregon. In 2016, customs authorities in San Diego seized 21,747 pounds of meth, almost 10 times what was apprehended in 2007. At border points in Arizona, California and Texas, agents seized 24 times as much.

In Montana, meth violations more than tripled between 2010 and 2015. In drug-related deaths in Oklahoma, meth is by far the No. 1 cause (oxycodone was a distant second). In Hawaii, where meth was first introduced in the United States, the number of people over 50 who said meth was their drug of choice has doubled in five years. In South Dakota, the attorney general has proclaimed an epidemic.

To counteract the falling price, drug cartels are actively pursuing new markets on the East Coast, according to the National Drug Threat Assessment released by the D.E.A. last fall.

Meth is carried across the border by people on foot, or hidden in cars and trucks. It can be converted to liquid, and has been smuggled in iced tea bottles, disguised as horse shampoo and hidden in tortillas.

The ingredient initially used to make it, ephedrine, was first synthesized in 1887 and later used to treat asthma. It was often used in the military and by truckers who needed to stay awake. For decades, United States lawmakers have been trying to curtail its use. But each time an ingredient was outlawed, something else took its place.

In 2007, Mexico cracked down on pseudoephedrine. The cartels reverted to using phenyl-2-propanone, known as P2P, a method popularized by biker gangs in the 1970s. Although it, too, is restricted and monitored, there are many ways to manufacture it.

Public health experts say little is being done to combat the surge in meth because it has been so overshadowed by opiates. And, there are fewer tools to combat meth than to combat opioids: There is nothing like Naloxone, which can reverse opioid overdoses, or methadone, which can stem opioid cravings.

Dr. Paul F. Lewis, the public health officer for the Portland metropolitan area, said the problem was complicated by the fact that many users take both drugs.

"We need to think about substance abuse much more broadly," Dr. Lewis said. "Eighty or 90 percent of heroin users are also using meth. It deserves more attention."

Eric, the former dancer, said the meth on the street was so strong that it worked best when used in combination with heroin to temper the effects.

"I have seen meth being used by people from age 12 to 90," he said. "It's a rush from all hell. Explosive. Intense. That goes away, and you're up for a long period of time. At first it's good. And then, after a while, it's too much."

CHAPTER 3

The Business of Addiction Treatment

With any crisis come attempts at a solution. In the case of the opioid crisis, its treatment has become a major business, with a range of treatment options emerging and a host of public and private interests looking to provide them. Along with the now-common overdose medication, naloxone, old and new addiction medicines play a significant role in treatment. In addition, there are many players in addiction treatment: clinics, law enforcement, the individuals impacted by addiction, and the numerous drug companies trying to sell their products.

At Clinics, Tumultuous Lives and Turbulent Care

BY DEBORAH SONTAG | NOV. 17, 2013

PITTSBURGH — The patient is an addict. His doctor is an addict, too. Over the last decade, both men hit their own versions of rock bottom. For the patient, it was the concrete floor of a jail where he writhed in withdrawal. For the doctor, it was the food stamp office where, his career as a child psychiatrist in tatters, he ashamedly sought help.

Then they both found buprenorphine, the patient as a user, the doctor as a prescriber. And because of that drug, an opioid used to treat opioid addiction, they both rebounded, even thrived.

The patient, Todd Smith, 27, who had developed a painkiller addiction because of a kidney disorder and — "I ain't gonna lie" — moved on to mainlining heroin, built a life with solidity: a car, a townhouse, a job as a mine safety inspector, a live-in fiancée and "knees worn out from praying."

The doctor, Allan W. Clark, 52, despite losing his Ohio medical license and being on probation in Pennsylvania for eight years, built a buprenorphine business so bustling that five doctors now work under him. His South Hills Recovery Project, tucked behind a 7-Eleven and beneath a hair salon, vibrates with the hubbub of the 600 addicts treated there.

Over the last couple of years, their fates have entwined, with Mr. Smith dependent on "Doc" for the treatment that keeps him stable at an out-of-pocket cost of $7,200 a year and Dr. Clark on "Smitty" and all the other cash-paying patients whose recovery he champions with an us-against-the-world fervor. They have shared, too, a keen awareness that their stability could be precarious.

"In recovery, you're constantly facing down your demons and dealing with the echoes of your past," Dr. Clark said. "But in the crazy world of buprenorphine, where this medicine that saves lives is harder to get and afford than the drugs that ruin lives, you're battling outside forces, too."

It is indeed a crazy world, or at least a vibrant, volatile subculture of people who see "bupe" as a lifeline, often difficult to reach, in an era when drug deaths outnumber those from car crashes. They scramble to find legitimate, affordable treatment even as buprenorphine is increasingly available on the street, with rising indicators of misuse and abuse tainting its reputation.

Buprenorphine was developed as a safer alternative to methadone for treating heroin and painkiller addiction, a take-home medication that could be prescribed by doctors in offices rather than dispensed daily in clinics. But in some areas a de facto clinic scene, unregulated, has developed, and it has a split personality — nonprofit treatment programs versus moneymaking enterprises built by individual doctors, some with troubled records.

The clinics serve as a crossroads where the tumultuous lives of recovering addicts converge and collide with a turbulent treatment environment.

Since March, The New York Times has visited and tracked the patients of two of the largest buprenorphine programs in this region, where addiction rates are high, for-profit clinics have proliferated, doctors go in and out of business and the black market is thriving.

Dr. Clark's hectic, cluttered office in suburban Pittsburgh is an entrepreneurial venture with heart where the rumpled doctor dresses in sweatsuits, the boundary between patients and employees is razor thin, the requirements are minimal and the tolerance for missteps is maximal.

"I know on the surface it might look like a pill mill," he said. "We're seeing a fair number of patients, and they're primarily receiving a prescription. But if you look deeper, you'll see that we don't use the medication in a vacuum. We encourage, we support, we don't judge. There's a kind of love."

Sixty miles away, the more formal, structured treatment center at West Virginia University in Morgantown sits atop a hill, ensconced in a hospital complex and presided over by Dr. Carl R. Sullivan III, a career addictionologist who wears a white lab coat and stands professorially at the front of a classroom when he meets his patients in groups: "Are you clean? How many meetings have you been to?" he asks them.

Dr. Sullivan, 61, primarily treated alcoholism until "a spectacular explosion of prescription opioid drugs" starting around 2000. He considered opioid addiction "a hopeless disease," with patients leaving rehab and then relapsing and sometimes dying, until he started prescribing Suboxone, the brand-name drug whose main ingredient is buprenorphine, as a maintenance therapy in 2004.

He became a paid treatment advocate for the manufacturer, Reckitt Benckiser, delivering, he estimated, 75 talks at $500 each. But, he said, "If the company didn't pay me a nickel, I'd still promote

A Breakthrough: Before Suboxone, Dr. Carl R. Sullivan III considered opioid addiction "a hopeless disease."

Suboxone because in 2013, it's the best thing that's happened for the opioid addict."

Dr. Sullivan is skeptical of the buprenorphine "empires" in Pittsburgh — though not of Dr. Clark specifically, whom he does not know — believing that they feed the black market and tar the medication's reputation. Dr. Clark, in turn, is skeptical of "ivory tower" addiction programs with rigid rules and of doctors who, in his view, collude with the pharmaceutical industry.

"Big Pharma is in it for the super profits; we should be in it for the patients," said Dr. Clark, who nonetheless became a buprenorphine doctor partly because he needed to dig himself out of a financial hole.

AN UNLIKELY SAVIOR

Tall and lumbering, his balding head covered by a plaid cap, Mr. Smith strode into Dr. Clark's office last spring with the familiarity of a clinic

V.I.P., somebody whose urine is so consistently clean that he does not need to have his "pee tests" observed.

"Hey, Smitty, good to see you, my friend," Dr. Clark said, propping his sneakered feet on his desk and swigging from his habitual can of Red Bull. By his side, a harness whip, a gift from a patient, sat beneath the framed diplomas hanging crookedly on the wall.

"Hey, Doc," Mr. Smith said, settling his 270-pound frame into an armchair. He had hurried back from a job building windmills in Alaska just in time to get his next month's prescription: four 8-milligram tablets a day, the highest dose recommended, that stave off withdrawal, eliminate his cravings for heroin, keep his mood balanced and alleviate his chronic pain.

Growing up in the hilltop town of Meyersdale — "Pennsylvania's High Point" — Mr. Smith had aspired to follow his grandfather into the family business. "All I wanted to do was towing, in my Pap's footsteps," he said.

A rare kidney condition, treated with surgery and potent painkillers, knocked him off course. After several years, he told his doctor that he wanted to wean himself off the pills.

He said: "The doctor stopped dead like I had my pants on backward, and said, 'You're admitting you're addicted?' I said, 'Well, it ain't no news flash.' " The doctor ripped up his prescription and threw it in the air.

Mr. Smith spent the next week "dope sick," shivering, sweating and vomiting. A friend proposed a solution: heroin, cheap and easy to find. "Things started going south," Mr. Smith said. Then his grandfather died, and he learned that the towing business would be sold.

"I went clean off my rocker," he said. To finance his habit, he burned through $12,000 in savings and finally drove off to sell the contents of his gun safe, including weapons of disputed ownership. A police officer was waiting when he returned to arrest him for theft. Agonizing on that jailhouse floor, he promised himself he would never use again.

LESLYE DAVIS / THE NEW YORK TIMES

Breaking A Cycle: Amanda Rogers with her family in Toronto, Ohio. She took in her niece and nephew after her sister died of drug abuse last year.

A week later, essentially under house arrest in the custody of his father, a corrections officer, he called Dr. Clark's office, crying.

"He saved my life," Mr. Smith said.

That was two years ago. In his session last spring, Mr. Smith told his unlikely savior: "I'm sort of pissed at you. I hear you've been shooting Airsoft without me." (The game involves fake guns and pellets.)

"Yeah, sorry, buddy," the doctor said. "I know you'd be into that. What we all do in getting better is to switch to different ways of getting our ya-yas out, right?"

They talked motorcycles. The doctor drives a Harley-Davidson Fat Boy. Mr. Smith fantasizes about "barreling down the highway on a Big Dog" but is in too much debt to buy one. "You know how it is," he said.

Dr. Clark nodded. "I thought losing my credit was the worst thing in the world, but it was the best thing in the world because now I'm living on a cash basis," he said. "Credit is a big scam, man. It uses our addictive nature against us: 'I want it now. I want it now.' "

Mr. Smith loves it when Dr. Clark talks to him addict to addict. "I've heard patients say he ain't no better than we are or he's just in it for the money," he said. "But I think being an addict makes him a better doctor. He's been in our shoes."

DEFENDING THE DISPARAGED

With tattoos commemorating his recovery, Dr. Clark runs the office with his girlfriend, Natalie Tombs, also a recovering addict. Emotive and animated, Ms. Tombs has festooned the walls with inspirational messages on butterflies and hearts and signs warning against sharing, trading or selling medication: "ANY PATIENT CAN BE SUBJECTED TO RANDOM PILL COUNTS."

The couple portray themselves as the defenders of a disparaged segment of society with which they commiserate. Their patients see them that way, too.

"As you know, my pharmacist thinks you're pretty much a joke, and he's not filling your prescriptions," one patient, James Markeley, said recently. "I brought one in, handed it to him and said, 'How long will it be?' He said, 'It won't be.' "

Dr. Clark giggled. "What'd he say again?" he said. "I'm an old hippie? I like that one."

It was not always so.

A graduate of the University of Cincinnati College of Medicine, Dr. Clark did a fellowship in child psychiatry at Yale, served as an Air Force doctor in Germany and then took a job at a Pennsylvania hospital.

In the late 1990s, unhappy and overwhelmed by his patient load, he prescribed himself Adderall, a stimulant. His mood improved, and he focused better. But he kept taking more to get the same effect. After two years, he was a wreck.

Dr. Clark checked himself into a rehabilitation program in 1999.

"I had to cold-turkey it," he said. "Withdrawal from amphetamines is different. It's much more tolerable than from opioids. After detox, though, the obsession and craving for the drug are similar. The relapse rates are similar. The triggers are similar. I had to learn to manage stress better, to rest better, to improve my self-esteem."

Dr. Clark also had to meet the demands of Pennsylvania's physician recovery program: therapy as well as five 12-step meetings and two random urine screens a week.

After a few sober years, he relapsed when his marriage was breaking up. He wrote himself a prescription for painkillers in his son's name. His wife notified his program advocate.

"Just how much pain is your son in?" the advocate asked.

In 2002, a second residential program gave him a diagnosis of depression and narcissistic personality disorder — he disagreed — and discharged him early with a poor prognosis. He agreed to take a reprieve from practicing medicine in Pennsylvania; Ohio suspended his license.

Deeply in debt, Dr. Clark was reduced to collecting food stamps until Pennsylvania let him return to medicine as a prison doctor in 2003.

That same year, after a positive drug test, Dr. Clark entered his third treatment program and promised himself it would be his last. He has been sober since, he said.

His troubles did not end with sobriety, though.

Pennsylvania suspended him for a month in 2010 because he failed to submit to three unannounced drug tests while on vacation. Ohio revoked his license in 2011 because he forged signatures verifying his attendance at 12-step meetings.

In 2008, a Reckitt Benckiser representative approached Dr. Clark at a children's hospital, saying: "There's this great medicine, Suboxone. Why not get certified? It doesn't take much, and it's a nice thing to add to your practice," he said.

Dr. Clark devised a treatment program based on federal guidelines, except he tailored it to what his working-class patients could afford. He mostly prescribed generic buprenorphine rather than the higher-priced Suboxone, which has an additive meant to deter abuse and is favored, though not mandated, by the guidelines.

And he established monthly, rather than more frequent, office visits unless patients violated the rules. He decided to "cut out the middleman" by declining to accept insurance and set his fee at $150 a visit, with a couples' price of $100 a person.

"I made sure my price was the lowest of any of the clinics, and that's why people liked us in the beginning," he said. "Many of my competitors were gouging them."

With his caseload limited to 100 by law, Dr. Clark quickly found himself turning away patients and searching for doctors who wanted to supplement their income by working part-time for him.

He hired the walk-in clinic doctor who monitored his urine drug screens, and an alternative medicine specialist who sees patients by Skype from Virginia. He also hired a 53-year-old internist shortly after a 25-year-old woman died of "acute combined drug toxicity" at the internist's home following an evening together at the Wicked Googly bar in Ligonier, Pa.

"He told me he was feeling some heat in his area and needed to get out of town for a while," Dr. Clark said.

After filing for bankruptcy protection with $1.5 million in debt early this year, the internist quit in May to run his own buprenorphine practice, saying he needed to make money fast, Dr. Clark said.

Dr. Clark scrambled to replace him so his patients would not be abandoned. They often are in this volatile field. Many of Dr. Clark's patients showed up on his doorstep after the authorities had put their previous doctors out of business.

'A CLASSY USER'

That happened with both Angela Scotchel, 25, and Amanda Rogers, 32. They are like before and after pictures. Ms. Scotchel, a former basketball star, is relatively fragile in her recovery, while Ms. Rogers appears firmly entrenched in hers despite a tempestuous personal life.

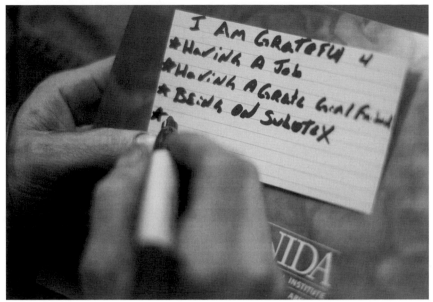

Taking Stock: Staff members at Dr. Clark's clinic encourage patients to list the things they are thankful for as they wait for counseling sessions.

In certain lights, Ms. Rogers, with her long blond hair and corn-flower blue eyes, looks like the cheerleader she was, before the people closest to her started dying from drugs and she developed a years-long habit.

"I never shot up; I always snorted," she said in March at her home in Toronto, Ohio. "I called myself a classy user. I always made sure the kids were taken care of and the bills were paid first."

In Steubenville, where Ms. Rogers grew up, drugs were every-where, and almost everybody in her life was an addict: her mother and stepfather, who suffered fatal overdoses; her younger sisters; her best friend; and her boyfriend.

"That town is like poison," she said. "I've probably lost close to 25 friends in the past 10 years."

She was 21 and devastated by her mother's death when she started seeking solace in the "nerve pills" her mother left behind. She became so dysfunctional that she lost custody of her first child to relatives, she said, then quit the pills, had a second child and sought help for back pain and fibromyalgia from a local doctor.

"I didn't know he was a pill pusher at the time," she said of the doctor, who was forced into retirement by the medical authorities in 2010. "He'd get people hooked and then kick them out to hunt for drugs on the street. And once you're on the street, heroin is cheaper than pills and lasts longer. I loved it."

Fearful she would end up killing herself, she found a Suboxone doctor she could afford and placed her first tablet under her tongue on Sept. 21, 2009. She has been clean since, she said proudly, despite traumas that tested her resolve.

In June 2012, her younger sister Tiffany was released from a court-mandated, abstinence-based rehabilitation program. She glowed, Ms. Rogers said. But returning to Steubenville, with temptation all around, proved too much for her. Ms. Rogers said, "She was crying and crying, bawling, saying, 'Mandy, I'm craving.' "

Within a week, Tiffany was dead at 26 of "acute cardiac and respiratory distress due to opioid abuse and dependency," her death certificate said.

"When I got that news, it was like with my mom," Ms. Rogers said. "I just wanted to get in bed and stop trying."

This time, though, she ran a household filled with the grief and need of her sister's traumatized children and of her own. So she coped. Then her Suboxone doctor lost his license for excessive narcotics prescribing, and she had to forage for medication on the street until Dr. Clark's office called in April with an unexpected opening.

Before Ms. Rogers's first appointment with him, her 2-year-old played boisterously as she described feeling achy and nauseous. Her buprenorphine supply had run out and withdrawal had begun.

"If it wasn't for my pain, I might tough it out," she said. "But if I went off the Subs, I'd have to go back on painkillers, and I'm not going back down that road."

A few hours later, clasping a heart pendant containing a vial of her sister's ashes, she told Dr. Clark with tearful defiance that she would not let her children or her sister's children follow in their parents' and grandparents' footsteps.

"I want to break that cycle," she said.

A BASKETBALL STAR'S FALL

Angela Scotchel was a first-generation user, but her family clung to her as she self-destructed. For her mother, Connie, that included lying by her side on the nights she overdosed to make sure she did not stop breathing. "You couldn't call an ambulance every single time," Connie Scotchel said.

Once a week, Mrs. Scotchel, a small-business owner with her husband, drives her daughter to Dr. Clark's office outside Pittsburgh from Morgantown to ensure she gets there and uses their hard-earned cash to pay the doctor and buy the medication. At home, Mrs. Scotchel keeps the buprenorphine in a locked safe and dispenses it dose by dose.

In her daily uniform of basketball shorts, Angela looks more like the point guard who used to squat 300 pounds than the scrawny addict who worked for an escort service to pay for her substantial heroin habit.

"I would never do anything like that sober in a million years," Angela said. "It was always men in their 40s, 50s and 60s, doctors and lawyers. Me being gay, it was especially disgusting. But I didn't care as long as I got high."

During her senior year of high school, playing a rival team in a packed gym, Angela stole a ball right before halftime, tore down the court, leapt for a layup and was smacked down by an opposing player. A hush blanketed the crowd. She had torn an anterior cruciate ligament. And though she recovered to start on a college team, she soon tore another ligament. After two surgeries, she felt she had lost her game. She also developed a taste for painkillers.

LESLYE DAVIS / THE NEW YORK TIMES

In Treatment: Jack Pierce with his daughter at Dr. Clark's clinic, where he got his Subutex prescription. "I really do believe it works," he said.

"A lot of people said I could go pro, play overseas," she said. "But I gave it all up for drugs. Every time I used, I hated myself. I felt like I had let everybody down. I wanted to die."

Over lasagna at their home, her parents talked about how bad things got: the times she disappeared, stole money from them, crashed cars, dangerously mixed heroin and Xanax. "I can't count the number of times the police and the municipality walked up these steps," Mrs. Scotchel said. "They assisted us with her overdoses time and time again. I'd have to follow her to the hospital. They'd shackle her. I'd be there all night waiting."

Putting down her fork, Angela Scotchel cried. "I went from a superstar to this lowdown dirty addict," she said.

She first tried Suboxone in Dr. Sullivan's clinic, which is 10 minutes from her home. But it made her ill. She thought she might be allergic to the additive in Suboxone and asked for plain buprenorphine. The clinic said no. She dropped out.

"They lived by the white coat there," her mother said, "while Dr. Clark is like one of the addicts."

Angela's heroin dealer stocked plain buprenorphine, so she tried it. It made her feel great, not sick, she said, so she found a doctor willing to prescribe it last year. After six months, she and her mother arrived at his office to find federal agents in windbreakers.

"We watched the D.E.A. go in and out, and I said, 'Angela, he's busted,' " Mrs. Scotchel said. "Poor Angela was crying, thinking she was going to get sick again."

They drove to Dr. Clark's office, even though they knew his waiting list was long. Seeing how distraught Angela was, the doctor took her on. Early this year, Angela confessed to Dr. Clark that she was injecting her buprenorphine and mixing it with Xanax. He threatened to discharge her unless she stopped immediately. She did.

Mrs. Scotchel insisted that Dr. Clark see her daughter weekly, even though they are uninsured and it adds $3,000 to the yearly cost. The doctor gives her a $20 discount for each Narcotics Anonymous meeting she writes up in her journal.

During her daughter's appointments, Mrs. Scotchel prefers to wait outside in her Subaru Forester, reading her Bible. "When I go in there, I gawk," she said. "It should be a reality show."

POLICING PRESCRIPTIONS

On a typical day last spring, Dr. Clark's waiting room was a tangle of mothers and babies, interlocked girlfriends and boyfriends, bikers in leather and miners with their names on their shirts. As conversation snippets made clear, they were wrestling with eviction notices and restraining orders, insurance headaches and custody problems, parole officers and abusive spouses.

"If he comes back and says, 'I've got a gun,' I'll load up my 12-gauge and it will be war!" said a patient with purple-streaked hair, mascara dripping down her cheeks.

Another woman, juggling two small children, car keys and a lit cigarette, told the office manager she was broke.

"I just gave you guys my last money, and I'm out of diapers and don't got gas," she said. The manager returned $25 to her and told her to get home safely.

Employees wandered about in shorts and flip-flops, shouting, "Can I have a pee cup, please?" Many are recovering addicts themselves, like Thomas Walleck, who staffs the drug testing station, in front of the Wall of Lost Souls — a collage of celebrities who died of overdoses.

Mr. Walleck, gentle and raspy-voiced, said he led patients to believe that his tests were all powerful so they would be forthright.

"I'll also tell them Doc has kicked out 180 people for dishonesty; I exaggerate," he said. "But we got to know if they're dirty for their own good. And if they admit it, it's good for the bottom line, too. Because then they have to come back in two weeks, and that's another $100."

Monitoring patients is a delicate task. Dr. Clark summons them for surprise pill counts; a sign in his office offers "CASH and FREE VISIT rewards for information leading to the prosecution of those who are engaging in illegal activity regarding their Suboxone/Subutex prescriptions."

Yet this policing clashes with the doctor's fierce instinct to take his patients' side and to confide in them about, say, his own reliance on antidepressants or his girlfriend's routine of reading recovery books while eating licorice in bed.

Ms. Tombs, the girlfriend, gets frustrated with his penchant for giving his patients second, third and fourth chances. After he wrote a 30-day buprenorphine prescription for a young man who had admitted to dealing cocaine, Ms. Tombs angrily drew 1,000 stick figures to illustrate those on their waiting list.

"I had to sleep in the office for three days," Dr. Clark said.

Usually the two are united against outside forces: the police who keep a too-watchful eye on their parking lot, the child protection workers who do not consider buprenorphine users drug free, the pharmacists who hassle their patients.

LESLYE DAVIS / NEW YORK TIMES

Commiseration: Dr. Allan W. Clark with Angela Scotchel, a recovering heroin addict, at his office near Pittsburgh. Like his patients, Dr. Clark has also struggled with addiction.

Dr. Clark has frequently felt under siege. He said a Reckitt Benckiser representative cautioned him that he was courting trouble with the authorities by prescribing generic buprenorphine and not Suboxone.

Last year, Dr. Clark wrote the Drug Enforcement Administration to ask whether he was indeed tempting fate.

A senior D.E.A. official responded that "what drug to prescribe, what formulation, what quantity" was a doctor's prerogative.

"It is unfortunate to learn that physicians in Western Pennsylvania have received incorrect information," the official wrote, "and that such misinformation may potentially be inhibiting legitimate treatment."

Feeling vindicated, Dr. Clark circulated the letter to pharmacists. But they were concerned, too, about the amounts he was prescribing. While within federal guidelines, his doses were on average twice those of Dr. Sullivan's.

Many of his patients, having flooded their bodies with potent opioids for years, need high doses, Dr. Clark said. Indeed, he noted, studies have shown higher treatment retention rates for people getting higher doses.

Dr. Sullivan, though, spoke with frustration about "prescribing wars" in Pittsburgh between "entrepreneurial doctors" who were "naively or maliciously overprescribing." "Which is terrible," he said. "Patients will take what they need and sell the rest. And once the medicine is on the street, for the D.E.A., it looks just like heroin: part of the problem. It blows back on all of us."

A STRUCTURED PROGRAM

Early this year, Dr. Sullivan invited the United States attorney for the Northern District of West Virginia to visit his clinic, which with its mushroom-colored walls and white-coated professionals inspires a kind of institutional hush.

The federal prosecutor, William J. Ihlenfeld II, said he was eager to be "enlightened" given that West Virginia has the country's second highest rate of overdose deaths and that a fifth of its babies have been exposed to drugs or alcohol in the womb.

"We've taken the approach in our office that we can't just arrest our way out of the problems we're facing with prescription drugs and heroin," Mr. Ihlenfeld said. Before his visit, he felt "somewhat close-minded about how effective something like this can be" given that he had "heard a lot of people in law enforcement complain" about buprenorphine.

What he saw inspired him, though, he said: "People benefiting, from a coal miner to a restaurant owner to somebody who had had ankle surgery and got sucked into addiction."

Dr. Sullivan's program, a showcase for buprenorphine treatment, is as regimented as Dr. Clark's is free form. New patients must attend one 90-minute session at the hospital plus four 12-step recovery meetings a week until they achieve 90 continuous days of sobriety, which usually takes half a year.

"There's no data to support it, but people who go to meetings get better," Dr. Sullivan said. "You can't just give addicts a pill, pat them on the head and expect them to turn things around for themselves. These people live very complicated and messy lives."

The new patients often inquire how long they will have to take buprenorphine. Once stable, though, they stop asking, realizing the answer is "maybe forever," Dr. Sullivan said.

"Forever seems like a nice alternative to dead," his patient Joellen Trippett, 48, said dryly.

At a staff meeting one day last spring, a case manager asked Dr. Sullivan how he wanted to handle a younger woman who was vigorously denying her pharmacy's report that she had sought to fill a prescription for Oxycodone.

"I guess we'll do an observed on her," Dr. Sullivan said, referring to a monitored urine test.

"An observed?" the case manager said. "How about a discharge?"

Relapses are plentiful — 12 of 50 patients that day — but patients are expelled only if they lie. Confronting the woman in her therapy group, Dr. Sullivan said that "surreptitious use of opioids is not permitted" and dismissed her with a prescription for one week of Suboxone.

Unlike Dr. Clark, Dr. Sullivan does not meet with patients individually. It would not be cost-effective; more than half of the clinic's patients are covered by Medicaid. Instead, he relies on therapists like Katie Chiasson, whose "advanced" group — those clean of drugs for at least a year and therefore required to come only monthly — was full of angst one day last spring.

Betty Jo Cumberledge, 47, announced in a trembling voice that she had just gotten a text from a fellow patient seeking to buy some of her Suboxone.

"Tell them that if they don't stop, you will expose them in group," Ms. Trippett said.

Ms. Chiasson asked how they could set boundaries.

"We all need to protect our medicine," Ms. Trippett said. "It gets stolen out of our cars and homes." She added that while selling Suboxone would be profitable, she did not want to return to the life she used to lead: "I don't want to be a cheat. I don't want to be a thief. I don't want to be a liar."

Chelsea Kennedy, 21, skinny and pregnant with her second child, reported that seven Suboxone dealers had been arrested in her town the previous week, and talked about her friend who gets a Suboxone prescription in Pittsburgh without even seeing the doctor — "and she's selling, shooting, buying, running the streets."

Ms. Cumberledge threw up her hands: "It's these kind of people who are hurting us."

A DISEASE'S TENTACLES

In late spring, Dr. Clark, still on probation, got an anxiety-provoking visit from a state medical investigator. Some pharmacists had complained about his prescribing practices, which led to the discovery that Dr. Clark had violated his 2010 suspension by continuing to write prescriptions for three buprenorphine patients he had not been able to place with other doctors.

When the investigator arrived, Mr. Smith was there. It made him nervous. He was already rattled, dealing with a job change and a custody battle, and did not want to contemplate losing Dr. Clark. "I'd be tossed right back out onto the street to buy drugs," he said.

Addiction is a tenacious disease with tentacles — family problems, legal problems, financial problems — that do not disappear with sobriety. Recovery has its zigs and zags, which many of the patients interviewed experienced this summer and fall.

Angela Scotchel, overwhelmed by anxiety about her future, constantly craved and sometimes gave in to her desire for Xanax. She also heard the siren call of opiates even as she set out to engage in life-affirming pursuits like lifting weights, working for her parents, dating.

"This one dealer called me today and said he got some fire in," she wrote in an email, referring to high-potency heroin. "I can't get it out of my head. I'm not gonna act on it, though. Just threw me off. I needed to tell someone about it."

Ms. Rogers rode a roller coaster of life changes. She broke up with her partner of 21 years and got involved with another man. She found a job as a cashier and lost it because of unreliable babysitters. She placed her late sister's children in a therapeutic foster home. She reluctantly moved back to Steubenville for lower-priced housing. She became pregnant with her fourth child.

Dr. Clark, meanwhile, prepared himself for the possibility that he could lose his license. He aggressively recruited other doctors, figuring he could manage the clinic. He watched the movie "Lincoln" twice; it helped him "deal with 'the negativity.' "

"I figure if Lincoln could fight for the rights of slaves during a time when many people thought this was practically criminal," he wrote in an email, "the least I can do is continue to fight for the rights of a few people suffering from the disease and stigma of addiction in my little part of the world."

At summer's end, though, his probation was lifted. He hired two New Jersey doctors, one a recovering addict, to see patients by Skype. His business grew fatter while he grew leaner, shedding 20 pounds and his sense of dread.

"I feel like I got de-stigmatized," Dr. Clark said. "Like now I got nothing to hide, nothing to fear, and there's hope for me and hope for all my patients. But we'll see."

Anti-Overdose Drug Becoming an Everyday Part of Police Work

BY J. DAVID GOODMAN AND ANEMONA HARTOCOLLIS | JUNE 12, 2014

AMID THE WEEKNIGHT BUSTLE of a Walmart parking lot in Centereach, N.Y., a young woman in a pickup truck had lost consciousness and was turning blue.

Her companion called 911. Possible drug overdose; come fast.

A Suffolk County police officer, Matthew Siesto, who had been patrolling the lot, was the first to arrive. Needles were visible in the center console; the woman was breathing irregularly, and her pupils had narrowed to pinpoints.

It seemed clear, Officer Siesto recalled of the October 2012 episode, that the woman had overdosed on heroin. He went back to his squad car and retrieved a small kit of naloxone, an anti-overdose medication he had only recently been trained to use in such circumstances. He prepared the dose, placed the atomizer in her nostril and sprayed.

"Within a minute," the officer said, "she came back."

Once the exclusive purview of paramedics and emergency room doctors, administering lifesaving medication to drug users in the throes of an overdose is quickly becoming an everyday part of police work amid a national epidemic of heroin and opioid pill abuse.

On Wednesday, Gov. Andrew M. Cuomo committed state money to get naloxone into the hands of emergency medical workers across New York, saying the heroin epidemic in the state was worse than that seen in the 1970s, and the problem is growing. Last month, the New York police commissioner, William J. Bratton, announced that the city's entire patrol force would soon be trained and equipped with naloxone. "Officers like it because it puts them in a lifesaving opportunity," Mr. Bratton said, suggesting that beat officers would carry it on their belts.

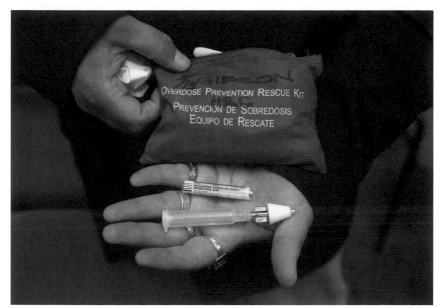

A rescue kit with naloxone.

New York is hardly alone. While the number of officers carrying the drug remains small for the moment — roughly two dozen of the country's 18,000 police departments have naloxone programs or are setting them up — police departments in cities as large as Boston and San Diego are preparing programs, as are more than 150 police forces across New York State.

"This is a huge change for policing," said Chuck Wexler, the executive director of the Police Executive Research Forum, an organization in Washington that conducts research on policing. "You're going to see this spread across the country."

The idea of having more police officers jump into this role is born of the practical reality that they are often the very first to arrive at the scene of an overdose, and based on its significant success in the small number of police departments that have tried it.

Among the first was Quincy, Mass., a city of about 93,000 residents just outside Boston that began equipping its 211 officers with the drug in 2010.

The speed of the change was striking: 90 residents died of drug overdoses in the 18 months before deploying naloxone; that dropped to nine in the year after officers began carrying it, said the police chief in Quincy, Paul Keenan.

"Once in a while, you'll get pushback from officers or the public — why are we saving junkies?" Chief Keenan said of the program, which has become a national model. "But our officers were going to too many houses to explain to families that their loved ones had passed away. We embraced it and we ran with it." Police officers there have so far reversed 252 overdoses, the chief said.

When someone has overdosed on an opiate drug like heroin, the brain begins to shut down respiration, eventually leading to coma and death. Naloxone, long available in emergency rooms and to paramedics, is an opiate blocker. "It takes the opiate out of the brain," said Dr. Merrill Herman, who heads psychiatric services at Montefiore Medical Center's methadone program in the Bronx.

In most cases, officers carry a nasal-spray device that is easier to use than an injection delivery system. Even with the restricted breathing that accompanies an overdose, the nasal spray is absorbed through the rich collection of blood vessels in the nostrils.

"It's really quite miraculous," said Dr. Mary Bassett, the New York City health commissioner. "Anyone who's ever reversed an overdose will never forget it. People wake up."

The restorative effects of the drug do not, however, resemble the scene from "Pulp Fiction," when a character played by Uma Thurman jolts back to life after receiving an injection of adrenaline.

Indeed, officers and emergency medical workers are occasionally faced with angry or violent reactions from addicts waking up and immediately craving drugs. "For somebody who's opiate dependent, they go into acute withdrawal," Dr. Bassett said. "It's not very pleasant."

James Brenker, 20, has been twice revived from an overdose by naloxone at Staten Island hospitals. "The second time is really a blur to me because I was really bad," he said. "I was legally dead." He recalled

Officer Matthew Siesto of the Suffolk County police in the parking lot in Centereach, N.Y., where he administer naloxone to revive a woman who had overdosed on heroin.

lashing out in the emergency room at his mother, Yvonne, who had called 911 after finding her son passed out on the front porch.

The medication caused an immediate chilling sensation as the heroin left his system. "Once I was reversed, I was instantly freezing cold," said Mr. Brenker, who entered rehab after his second naloxone experience last year and has since been clean. "Then your addiction automatically kicks back in. You're thinking, where do I get my next fix?"

In New York, the city health department worked with the Police Department to assist in the training of officers participating in a pilot program on Staten Island, where at least six overdoses have been reversed by the police this year. The expansion, giving 19,500 kits to officers in all precincts, is part of a $5 million program by the state attorney general, Eric T. Schneiderman, to put naloxone in the hands of all police officers in New York State.

The training involves teaching officers to recognize someone suffering from an overdose, including signs like pinpoint pupils, drowsiness, sedation, mental clouding and abnormal breathing.

The dose carried by officers is generally effective for about 45 minutes to an hour, so victims must still be taken to the hospital to be stabilized, usually a process of a few hours. Though some are told about treatment options at that point, they are free to leave.

There are no side effects if the antidote is administered to someone who is not overdosing, or is overdosing from a non-opiate, such as cocaine or a prescription medication like Xanax. It will not reverse that type of overdose. Dr. Bassett said she was not worried about the potential for the police to make mistakes. "This is a safe drug," she said. "There is no downside."

As in other aspects of police work, officers administering naloxone in places where programs have begun would be indemnified from legal liability, officials said. Some states have passed laws authorizing officers as well as some community members to carry and use the antidote.

Despite the obvious benefits of the drug, there is still some debate over its wide implementation. Health and treatment officials caution that naloxone alone will not cure an epidemic of overdoses that claims thousands of lives each year. Users brought back from overdose often do not clamor for treatment.

Dr. Lewis Nelson, medical toxicologist in the department of emergency medicine at New York University School of Medicine, acknowledged that the antidote certainly would save lives, but said it carried some risks. Giving it to an addict will induce withdrawal, which can cause extreme anxiety, uncontrolled anger and violent behavior. Some people may try to control the withdrawal by taking more drugs.

"Precipitated" withdrawal is also associated with physical symptoms like vomiting and diarrhea, he said, and can lead to marked increases in blood pressure and pulse, which can cause seizure, stroke, pulmonary edema or heart attack.

There is also concern that some heroin users may become more careless, knowing that police officers will be carrying an antidote.

A 22-year-old man who was revived by naloxone on Staten Island two weeks ago is "treating the whole thing nonchalantly," his mother said the next day. "I don't think he realizes the severity of what happened, which is not a good sign."

Indeed, some police chiefs speak to the frustration that within hours of a naloxone reversal, some users are back on the street with "the same compelling addiction and no intervention," said David A. Paprota, the police chief in Lacey Township, N.J. "Most often go right back to using."

For Officer Siesto on Long Island, his experience in the Walmart parking lot was his second time reviving a person with naloxone in a little over a month after Suffolk County began a pilot program in 2012 to equip police officers with the drug.

The officer, 32, has since made three more "saves" — though one of those included the same young woman from the pickup truck.

"I saved that girl's life less than 30 days later. A 911 call at her house," he said. "I was a little upset that she's still using."

Officer Siesto said that he had recently seen the woman, now 20, around the area where he patrols.

Her mother has received training, he said, and now carries naloxone herself.

Naloxone Saves Lives, but Is No Cure in Heroin Epidemic

BY KATHARINE Q. SEELYE | JULY 27, 2016

PORTLAND, ME. — A woman in her 30s was sitting in a car in a parking lot here last month, shooting up heroin, when she overdosed. Even after the men she was with injected her with naloxone, the drug that reverses opioid overdoses, she remained unconscious. They called 911.

Firefighters arrived and administered oxygen to improve her breathing, but her skin had grown gray and her lips had turned blue. As she lay on the asphalt, the paramedics slipped a needle into her arm and injected another dose of naloxone.

In a moment, her eyes popped open. Her pupils were pinpricks. She was woozy and disoriented, but eventually got her bearings as paramedics put her on a stretcher and whisked her to a hospital.

Every day across the country, hundreds, if not thousands, of people who overdose on opioids are being revived with naloxone. Hailed as a miracle drug by many, it carries no health risk; it cannot be abused and, if given mistakenly to someone who has not overdosed on opioids, does no harm. More likely, it saves a life.

As a virulent opioid epidemic continues to ravage the country, with 78 people in the United States dying of overdoses every day, naloxone's use has increasingly moved out of medical settings, where it has been available since the 1970s, and into the homes and hands of the general public.

But naloxone, also known by the brand name Narcan, has also had unintended consequences. Critics say that it gives drug users a safety net, allowing them to take more risks as they seek higher highs. Indeed, many users overdose more than once, some multiple times, and each time, naloxone brings them back.

Advocates argue that the drug gives people a chance to get into treatment and turn their lives around and that there is no evidence

Police officers, firefighters and paramedics responding last month to a report of a possible overdose in Portland, Me.

naloxone increases the use of opiates. And, they say, few addicts knowingly risk needing to be revived, since naloxone ruins their high and can make them violently ill.

With drug overdoses now killing more people than car crashes in most states, lawmakers in all but three — Kansas, Montana and Wyoming — have passed laws making naloxone easier to obtain. Its near-universal availability reflects the relatively humane response to the opioid epidemic, which is based largely in the nation's white, middle-class suburbs and rural areas — a markedly different response from that of previous, urban-based drug epidemics, which prompted a "war on drugs" that led to mass incarceration, particularly of blacks and Hispanics.

This more compassionate response has been on display this week at the Democratic National Convention in Philadelphia. Speakers there have talked about addiction and the need for more accessible treatment, and a call by Senator Jeanne Shaheen of New Hampshire for all emergency responders to carry naloxone drew applause from the delegates.

Nonprofit organizations began distributing naloxone to drug users in the mid-1990s, but most of the state laws making it more accessible have been enacted only in the last few years. Between this and so-called good Samaritan laws that provide immunity to people who call 911 to report an overdose, the chances are much greater now that someone who overdoses will be saved and given medical attention instead of left for dead or sent to jail.

The federal government still requires a prescription for naloxone, but that is under review by the Food and Drug Administration, which has also approved a Narcan nasal spray that is easier to administer and is growing increasingly popular.

There is no question that the nation's death toll from heroin and prescription opioids would be significantly higher without naloxone. Prince, the pop superstar, is just one of those who were saved by it. After he overdosed on Percocet, an opiate painkiller, on his airplane in April, the plane made an emergency landing, and he was revived on the tarmac with naloxone — only to overdose on fentanyl six days later and die when no one was around to administer naloxone.

In 2014, in Maine alone, 208 people died from overdoses. That year, emergency responders saved 829 lives with naloxone. But that was just a fraction of those saved here, as most uses go unreported. In 83 percent of cases, according to a national survey last year by the Centers for Disease Control and Prevention, naloxone is given by other drug users, the people most likely to be on the scene, not by emergency responders.

But in Maine this spring, Gov. Paul LePage, a Republican, questioned the effectiveness of naloxone and vetoed legislation that would have increased access to it.

"Naloxone does not truly save lives; it merely extends them until the next overdose," Mr. LePage wrote in his veto message in April. "Creating a situation where an addict has a heroin needle in one hand and a shot of naloxone in the other produces a sense of normalcy

Sarah Connolly at her home in Falmouth, Me., last month. Ms. Connolly, 26, overdosed seven years ago in the bathroom of a Burger King in Michigan and was revived with naloxone.

and security around heroin use that serves only to perpetuate the cycle of addiction."

Yet most users loathe naloxone's effects. By blocking opiate receptors, it plunges them into withdrawal and makes them "dope sick," craving more heroin or pills.

"I hate it," said Melissa Tucci, 44, a heroin user here who has been revived seven times. "When I start withdrawing, I vomit, you get diarrhea, you sweat profusely, your nose will run, you sneeze and have runny eyes, and you ache so bad you can't even walk."

She said she has overdosed so often not because she relied on naloxone to save her, but rather because she underestimated how potent the heroin was. And she said she keeps using heroin to avoid the agony of withdrawal.

The Maine Legislature easily overrode the governor's veto. According to the Network for Public Health Law, Maine is now one of 34 states with what is called a standing order, essentially a prescription that makes naloxone available to the general public.

Still, Mr. LePage gave voice to the troubling reality that some people repeatedly overdose, and can seem stubbornly resistant to help.

"They're usually very angry when we bring them around," said Deputy Chief John Everett of the Portland Fire Department. "One kid yelled at me, 'You think this will make me stop doing drugs?' I said, 'No, the only thing that will make you stop doing drugs is a body bag.' "

On the other hand, Sarah Connolly, 26, said she was alive because of naloxone. Seven years ago she was revived after overdosing in the bathroom of a Burger King in Michigan. "Most of my veins were so deteriorated from using that they had to give it to me in my hand," she said recently at a training session here on how to administer naloxone. She said that after overdosing, she left an emergency room against medical advice and went out to find more heroin.

She continued to use heroin, but stopped cold when she became pregnant. Now she is unrecognizable from her days of addiction. She moved to Maine, married her son's father, is pregnant with their second child, and is studying to be a high school English teacher.

"I have a real sense of purpose now," she said. "I believe I'm a miracle because I had a second chance."

Gov. Tom Wolf of Pennsylvania, a Democrat, said in a recent interview that the only responsible approach to the epidemic ravaging his state was to make naloxone widely available and provide more treatment. Pennsylvania is one of the states with a standing order for naloxone.

"This is a disease, not a moral failing," Mr. Wolf said.

Dr. Alexander Y. Walley, an addiction medicine specialist at Boston Medical Center, said arguing that naloxone encourages riskier drug use was like saying that seatbelts encourage riskier driving.

"A person with an opioid use disorder is by definition using despite harmful consequences," Dr. Walley said. That aside, he said, "receiving naloxone not only reverses the overdose, it also reverses the euphoria and withdrawal relief that the opioid user is seeking. Thus, it is only used as a last resort."

Dr. Mark Publicker, an addiction medicine specialist in Portland, said that repeated overdoses were often the result of increasingly potent heroin, especially when combined with drugs like fentanyl and sedatives, producing a lethal cocktail.

"While your psychological tolerance becomes greater, your cardiorespiratory tolerance doesn't," he said. "You keep pushing the limit because your reward threshold has become impossibly high."

Naloxone can start to wear off 20 to 30 minutes after it is administered and dissipate entirely after 90 minutes. The withdrawal from the opiate can be so brutal that it often drives people to use heroin again right away.

"I had a woman who overdosed three times in one day," said Zoe Odlin-Platz, a community health promotion specialist at the India Street needle exchange here. After the third overdose, she said, the woman broached the possibility of seeking treatment.

The bigger problem, advocates say, is the dearth of available treatment, particularly for people without insurance. Nevertheless, Portland paramedics make every effort to take revived drug users to a hospital, and hope that in those moments after being revived, they might decide to seek help.

"People are vulnerable at that point, and I ask them if they want to talk," said Oliver Bradeen, a substance use disorder liaison for the Portland Police Department, who responds to most emergency overdose calls. And, he said, "sometimes the universe comes together and it works out."

But sometimes it doesn't.

Bruce Carleton, a veteran paramedic with the Portland Fire Department, was among those who responded last month when the woman in the parking lot overdosed. He talked her into going to the hospital, but when he went by her room later on, her bed was empty.

Haven for Recovering Addicts Now Profits From Their Relapses

BY LIZETTE ALVAREZ | JUNE 20, 2017

DELRAY BEACH, FLA. — It was the kind of afternoon that cold-weary tourists revel in as they sip mojitos near the beach — a dazzling sun, a sky so blue it verged on Photoshopped and weather fit for flip-flops. But the young visitor from Arkansas, curled up into a ball near the sidewalk, had a better reason to be grateful. He was alive.

"You are overdosing on heroin," Sean Gibson, a paramedic captain with the Delray Beach Fire-Rescue, had told him earlier this year, after the man fell off his bike, hit a chain-link fence and collapsed, blood trickling down his face. Mr. Gibson sprayed Narcan, an opiate blocker, up the man's nose as he lay on his back and, before long, the man — who had shot up heroin at a recovery group home — sat up, polite and embarrassed. "Thanks, guys," he said, before being taken to the hospital as a precaution.

In a nation awash in opioids, there are few, if any, places where this kind of scene plays out more often than this artsy beach town of 15 square miles. Here, heroin overdoses long ago elbowed out car crashes and routine health issues as the most common medical emergencies. Last year, Delray paramedics responded to 748 overdose calls; 65 ended in fatalities. In all, Palm Beach County dealt with 5,000 overdose calls.

Unlike other places in the United States that have been clobbered by the opioid crisis, most of the young people who overdose in Delray Beach are not from here. They are visitors, mostly from the Northeast and Midwest, and they come for opioid addiction treatment and recovery help to a town that has long been hailed as a lifeline for substance abusers. But what many of these addicts find here today is a crippled and dangerous system, fueled in the past three years by insurance fraud, abuse, minimal oversight and lax laws. The result in Palm Beach County has been the rapid proliferation of troubled treatment

Paramedics in Delray Beach, Fla., helping a young man after reviving him from a heroin overdose in February. Last year, Palm Beach County dealt with 5,000 overdoses.

centers, labs and group homes where unknowing addicts, exploited for insurance money, fall deeper into addiction.

"We have these people sending us their children to get healthy," said Dave Aronberg, the state attorney for Palm Beach County, who established a sober homes task force to combat the problem, "and they are leaving in ambulances and body bags."

THWARTING RECOVERY

When several inpatient treatment centers, drawn by low taxes and warm weather, opened their doors here to addicts more than 35 years ago, it seemed a godsend to substance abusers. Soon, other centers, mostly legitimate, followed. Recovering addicts lived together after treatment in supervised apartments or single-family homes. The residences were known as sober homes, where addicts could recover far from temptations and drug-abusing friends back home.

Addicts attended outpatient therapy, found jobs and buoyed each other as they waded back into everyday life. Many stayed in Delray Beach, drawing more addicts as word spread. In time, Narcotics Anonymous and Alcoholics Anonymous meetings were almost as easy to find as a cup of coffee; today there are at least 150 meetings a week. Experts called the treatment and sober house system the Florida Model, and it spread quickly across the country.

"Sober home, sober home, sober home, sober home," said Marc Woods, a housing inspector for the city, as he gestured out the car window along one block of single-family houses. He turned the corner. "Sober home, sober home."

Hundreds of sober homes — some reputable, many of them fraud mills and flop houses for drug users — sprawl across Delray Beach and several surrounding cities. No one knows exactly how many exist because they do not require certification, only city approval if they want to house more than three unrelated people. Hoping for a fresh start, thousands of young addicts from outside Florida wind up here in places that benefit from relapse rather than the recovery they advertise.

"The state of Florida licenses haircutters, yet we don't license any of the people involved in the supervision of young adults suffering from substance abuse disorder, far away from home, without means," said Cary Glickstein, the mayor of Delray Beach. "These desperate patients and family members are getting exploited and abused."

Why did this happen? For one thing, Florida, a state famous for insurance fraud, disdains regulation and was ground zero for the prescription drug epidemic. But the proliferation of fraudulent sober homes was in part also the result of two well-intentioned federal laws. First came a 2008 law that gave addicts more generous insurance benefits; then the Affordable Care Act, which permits adults under 26 to use their parents' insurance, requires insurance companies to cover people with pre-existing conditions and allows for multiple drug relapses.

A former motel, now a sober house, in Delray Beach. Hundreds of sober homes are scattered throughout Delray Beach and nearby cities. No one knows exactly how many exist because the homes do not require certification.

The result was a whole new category of young addicts with access to insurance benefits. This gave rise to a new class of abusive operator, as painstakingly chronicled in The Palm Beach Post: the corrupt sober house owner. Many drug treatment centers — which also treated inpatients — started paying sober-home owners "bonuses" from insurance money and fees for referring outpatients to their centers while they underwent therapy, according to law enforcement, a grand jury report and court records.

This is illegal. Sober homes, which are not covered by insurance, can get thousands of dollars a month for each recovering addict, in large part from treatment providers, law enforcement and city officials said.

Much of it goes into the owners' pockets. But it is also used to pay rent so patients can live free and to provide perks that lure patients from other sober houses: manicures, mopeds, gym memberships and, worst of all, drugs. Relapses are welcome because they restart the benefits clock.

To increase profits, many treatment centers and labs overbill insurance companies for unnecessary tests, including of urine, blood and DNA. Some have billed insurance companies thousands of dollars for a urine test screen. Patients often unnecessarily undergo multiple urine tests a week.

Cracking down has proved difficult. Florida does not regulate sober homes, and federal disability and housing anti-discrimination laws offer strong protections to recovering addicts who live in them. Sober houses are categorized as group homes for the disabled. This has complicated arrests, cases and lawsuits, although some treatment centers, lab and sober-house owners in the area have been prosecuted on state or federal charges for patient brokering and money laundering, the result of the Sober Homes Task Force. In some of the worst cases, women were held captive, raped and drugged in sober homes.

Some help may be on the way. After months of sidestepping the issue, Gov. Rick Scott declared an opioid public health emergency in May, freeing up $27 million in federal money for prevention, treatment and recovery. And the Florida Legislature approved a bill that will stiffen penalties for patient brokering and fraudulent marketing.

Few in Delray Beach have escaped unscathed: not the addicts or their parents who send them here, often lured by well-paid recruiters. Not the residents who find overdosed young adults on their lawns. Not the county medical examiner who, overwhelmed by opioid deaths, stopped doing autopsies on car accident victims last year. And not the city, which has spent millions of extra dollars on the surge of heroin addicts from out of state.

ADDICTS VS. THE 'BAD GUYS'

Sober homes here are everywhere. They are in wealthy beach-side enclaves, middle-class strongholds and gentrifying neighborhoods.

Benita Goldstein, an Osceola Park resident, bought a house simply to shut down the sober home that occupied it. "We are trying to recover from the recovery homes," she said.

Sometimes whole apartment buildings are converted into sober homes. The houses can be gorgeous; they can also be grim. Most of those are in low-income neighborhoods, where property is cheap, drug dealers plentiful and residents less inclined to make a fuss.

Emanuel Dupree Jackson Jr. lives in a largely Haitian and African-American neighborhood among people who got knocked sideways by drugs, mostly crack, long ago. Like him, many had been arrested or had landed in prison for dealing. Or they withered away after using. Or they got killed for tangling with the unforgiving rules of street dealing.

The last thing this area needed was hundreds of white "hard-core junkies" from out of state, he said. But sober houses opened anyway, attracted by cheap housing and residents who are wary of authority.

Dealers soon sized up their new customers and stocked up on the drug of choice: heroin. Relapses and overdoses skyrocketed, particularly after potent synthetic opioids like fentanyl and Carfent-anil hit the street. But addicts, who seldom have drugs on them, get a trip to the hospital. Dealers, if caught, get a trip to jail.

"My cousin will sell the drugs to them and go to jail, and the white people who are in the sober homes are protected," said Mr. Jackson, 33, who runs a nonprofit for low-income youth. "But what came first? You put the heroin users here, with poor people, with a history of drugs and violence, with no regulation."

"They are known addicts," he added, "but we are still the bad guys."

Closer to the beach, in Osceola Park, a gentrifying area, residents are no less upset. It's not drug treatment they oppose — it's the mind-boggling number of poorly run sober houses.

They find needles in their yards. The town soundtrack is unrelenting siren wails. With six to 12 people living in a house, noise is unavoidable. Property crime last year was up 19 percent from 2015. The "new homeless" — as the police call addicts who get booted from sober houses once insurance money runs out — are living on the streets.

"We are trying to recover from the recovery homes," said Benita Goldstein, whose house in Palm Trail sits behind a sober home and who bought another house here simply to shut down the sober home that occupied it. "The affliction is everywhere."

Lynn Korp lives a stone's throw from Delray's popular main street, Atlantic Avenue, which hums with packed restaurants and galleries. One morning, Ms. Korp, an artist, spotted a man on the ground behind her house. A needle jutted from his arm.

"He was deceased," she said, still troubled by the memory. "I don't even know what that gentleman's name was, and I still think about his mother and siblings."

Residents blame the city, in part, for the sober-house sprawl. Delray Beach officials are so afraid of lawsuits that they are paralyzed, Ms. Goldstein said.

Mayor Glickstein, who was just re-elected, said that federal anti-discrimination laws protecting people in recovery are so strict that cities that try to curtail sober houses routinely lose big money lawsuits. It happened in nearby Boca Raton.

One remedy is in the works. In November, two federal agencies issued guidance on the problem, granting cities some wiggle room to use zoning and other tools to control the proliferation. The city is now drafting an ordinance that it hopes will do just that.

"The laws were frankly never intended to be used for the ware-housing of people suffering substance abuse disorders," Mr. Glickstein said. "They have been turned on their head for profit."

A PIPELINE TO RELAPSE

For many addicts, living in sober homes was a pipeline to relapse. Amanda Ramalho, a drug rehab veteran from Lowell, Mass., chose a reputable treatment center in South Florida in 2015 — a place far from the snow, where new beginnings didn't seem so far-fetched.

But the sober homes, meant to ease her recovery, did the opposite.

"Everyone was always high, and when people are in there getting high, you run around with them getting high," said Ms. Ramalho, 26, who returned home in 2016 and is now sober after spinning out of control in Delray Beach. "It's supposed to be the biggest recovery capital, but it's really the biggest relapse capital."

She overdosed three times. Twice she wound up in the hospital. Once, she nearly died after the sober house supervisor brought in heroin, she said, which is not uncommon in some sober homes. A friend well versed in overdose triage saved her with CPR because calling fire rescue is a last resort. It gives paramedics and police officers entree into the sober houses, which could lead to code violations or arrests if drugs are found.

"Usually people wake up," she said. Inside a sober house, "they are ready for people to overdose."

Even the white vans, called "druggie buggies," that take people to therapy are not off limits. Ms. Ramalho said she looked back during one ride and saw a man overdosing. They changed plans: "We had to carry him into the hospital."

Paramedics and firefighters, like the ones at Delray Beach Fire Station 1, see it all. During peak periods, they can race to 20 overdose calls in a day.

"You look at their IDs," said Kris Scheid, 42, a driver engineer. "And they are all clean-cut. Then you look at them now, and they are destroyed. You say, 'Is this the same person?' "

Sometimes, they treat the same person several times in a single day. Or they rescue several people in a single place who had shared a bad batch. Almost always the victims are under 26, white and from out of state. Around town, they are called the "zombies."

"You throw a rock in all four directions and you can hit someone who had OD'd, will OD or did heroin today," said Capt. Chris Zidar, 44.

Neal de Jesus, a former fire chief who is serving as acting city manager, said he was so worried about the toll of so many overdoses and deaths that he ordered routine counseling for firefighters and paramedics. The police department brought in counselors, too.

"I have more than 30 years in the business," he said. "My firefighters have seen more death in two years than I have seen in my entire career."

With so much work for emergency personnel, the police and fire departments have been on a hiring spree.

At the morgue, the medical examiner, Dr. Michael D. Bell, saw the jump in opioid deaths firsthand in 2015. The number climbed even more sharply last year, when ultra-potent heroin laced with synthetics hit the streets. His workload increased 25 percent both years. Last year, 596 people died from opioids in the county. They added a pathologist. Now he needs two more.

Even he, a man used to the constancy of death, said he was taken aback.

"It has really surprised me, how many people die," Dr. Bell said. "It truly is an epidemic much like when people were dying of AIDS, at first."

Study Finds Competing Opioid Treatments Have Similar Outcomes

BY ABBY GOODNOUGH AND KATE ZERNIKE | NOV. 14, 2017

WASHINGTON — A long-awaited study has found that two of the main medications for treating opioid addiction are similarly effective, a finding likely to intensify the hard-fought competition between drugmakers seeking to dominate the rapidly expanding opioid treatment market.

The study, funded by the federal government, compared Vivitrol, which comes in a monthly shot and blocks the effects of opioids, and Suboxone, which is taken daily in strips that dissolve on the tongue and contains a relatively mild opioid that helps minimize withdrawal symptoms and cravings.

Researchers found that 52 percent of those who started on Vivitrol relapsed during the 24-week study, compared with 56 percent of those who started on Suboxone.

But the study, conducted with 570 adults addicted mostly to heroin, also found a substantial hurdle for Vivitrol. Because the medication can be started only after a person is completely detoxed from opioids — a process that can take over a week — more than a quarter of the study participants assigned to Vivitrol dropped out before being able to take their first dose. Suboxone can be started shortly after withdrawal symptoms begin, and only six percent of those assigned to take that drug dropped out before taking an initial dose.

Drug manufacturers have been competing fiercely to develop and market medications to treat opioid addictions, which have propelled a steep increase in the number of drug deaths in the United States. Last year, 64,000 Americans died from drug overdoses, up 22 percent from the previous year.

There is significant money at stake. Under a law passed by Congress in 2016, the Trump administration is sending $1 billion to states to deal with the epidemic over the next two years, with directions to prioritize so-called medication assisted treatment. Mr. Trump's opioid commission recently implored Congress to swiftly appropriate more money.

Suboxone, made by Indivior, is the older, cheaper, and much more widely studied and used of the two medications. The manufacturer of Vivitrol, Alkermes, has tried to catch up by marketing its drug as a cleaner alternative, emphasizing that Vivitrol is the only federally approved addiction medication that does not contain an opioid.

Vivitrol is also the most expensive addiction medication, with Medicaid paying about $500 per shot, according to Alkermes, and private insurers paying $1,000. Suboxone tends to cost a third to half as much. Another addiction medication approved by the Food and Drug Administration, methadone, is much cheaper, but people who take it have to go to specially licensed clinics for their daily dose. The study focused on Vivitrol and Suboxone because both can be prescribed by primary care doctors, although a federal waiver is needed to prescribe Suboxone.

Using free samples and millions of dollars in political donations, Alkermes has pushed for the use of Vivitrol in drug courts and jails, where Suboxone is often not allowed. Vivitrol has won fans among many law enforcement officials who see Suboxone as simply replacing one addiction for another. Suboxone is also more likely to be diverted into a black market, though addiction experts say that people who use it are trying to stave off withdrawal, not get high.

But Alkermes' strategy has drawn attention from lawmakers and law enforcement officials concerned that it is encouraging misconceptions about Suboxone as it tries to promote Vivitrol.

Last week, Senator Kamala Harris of California, a Democrat, announced a Senate committee investigation into the company's "sales, marketing and educational" tactics, which she said had attempted to artificially boost sales by stigmatizing treatments like Suboxone.

Advertising for Vivitrol on a subway car in Brooklyn. Marketing for the drug has shifted into high gear.

"It is crucial that treatment approaches rest on sound science and the best judgment of medical professionals — not the marketing and lobbying prowess of the pharmaceutical industry," she wrote in a letter to Alkermes.

Alkermes also recently acknowledged in a filing with the Securities and Exchange Commission that it is cooperating in an investigation by the Justice Department, though it did not say what the focus was.

Suboxone, which has more market share than any other addiction medication, has also come under scrutiny. Its maker has been sued by 43 state attorneys general who say the company schemed to block generic competition by conspiring with another company to create a slightly different delivery system for the drug.

In a recent earnings report, the company said it was discussing a resolution to a federal investigation regarding its marketing and promotion practices.

The new study, published on Tuesday in The Lancet, was only the second to compare the drugs, and the first in the United States. A study conducted in Norway and released last month had similar results, but it was shorter and included fewer patients.

The study's authors downplayed the drop-off in the patients assigned to Vivitrol, saying that the difficulty detoxing is already well-known. The pressing question, they argued, was whether the two drugs worked equally well.

"The main finding in my view is the relatively equivalent safety and effectiveness of these two medications," said Dr. John Rotrosen, a psychiatry professor at New York University School of Medicine and the study's lead investigator.

But in a commentary that the Lancet published along with the study, David Lott, a professor at the University of Illinois College of Medicine, raised concerns about the problem of getting through detox to start Vivitrol, noting that most study participants who failed to detox long enough to start Vivitrol did relapse.

Dr. Rotrosen and Dr. Joshua Lee, a co-author of the study and an associate professor at New York University School of Medicine, have both led or participated in previous studies for which Alkermes provided medication or funding. Two of the other authors also reported receiving research support and in one case, consulting fees from Alkermes. Indivior donated the Suboxone for the study.

Twenty-eight overdoses were reported during the study, which ran from January 2014 through January 2017. Nine occurred in people who never started the medications. Overdose rates among those who took at least one dose did not differ between the two treatment groups, and most occurred well after the last dose of medication.

Dr. Nora Volkow, the director of the National Institute on Drug Abuse, which sponsored the study, said that for those in danger of relapsing before they can fully detoxify, doctors should promptly prescribe Suboxone or another drug containing buprenorphine, its main ingredient.

In a statement, Alkermes said the study was additional evidence to support more widespread use of Vivitrol, and called its drug "an entirely different approach" to medication-assisted treatment.

The company's chief medical officer, Craig Hopkinson, said the study underscored the importance of detoxification before starting treatment, and noted that the company is working to develop additional drugs that help with detox.

Neither medication is nearly as widely used as it should be, addiction experts say. Although research has found that medication-assisted treatment reduces overdose deaths and relapse, 85 percent of counties have no opioid treatment program that provides it, according to the president's commission.

Dr. Volkow said she hoped the study would dispel misperceptions that some doctors have about Vivitrol, including that patients don't tolerate it well and that it doesn't work as well with cases of severe addiction. Now, she said, researchers should focus on the most effective ways to detox people so they can start Vivitrol and on determining which medication is best for each individual patient.

"It's extremely important," she said. "What patient characteristics can lead me as a physician to determine that this particular individual will do better on one of these medications than the other?"

"We have it for every other area of medicine, but not for the treatment of opioid use disorders."

Opioid Addiction Knows No Color, but Its Treatment Does

BY JOSE A. DEL REAL | JAN. 12, 2018

ON A STREET lined with garbage trucks, in an industrial edge of Brooklyn, dozens of people started filing into an unmarked building before the winter sun rose. Patients gather here every day to visit the Vincent Dole Clinic, where they are promised relief from their cravings and from the constant search for heroin on the streets.

Robert Perez exited the clinic on a recent Wednesday and walked toward the subway, along the Gowanus Canal. Within the clinic's antiseptic blue walls, he had just swallowed a red liquid from a small plastic cup. The daily dose of methadone helps Mr. Perez, 47, manage withdrawal symptoms as he tries to put decades of drug abuse behind him.

"I wish I didn't have to come here every day, but I have to," Mr. Perez said outside the clinic. "If you don't do it, you're sick. You wake up sick."

Mr. Perez is not alone. For recovering users without money or private health insurance, these clinics are often the only option to get their lives on track, even as less cumbersome alternatives have become available for those who can pay for it.

In New York City, opioid addiction treatment is sharply segregated by income, according to addiction experts and an analysis of demographic data provided by the city health department. More affluent patients can avoid the methadone clinic entirely, receiving a new treatment directly from a doctor's office. Many poorer Hispanic and black individuals struggling with drug addiction must rely on these highly regulated clinics, which they must visit daily to receive their plastic cup of methadone.

Mr. Perez expressed gratitude at the chance to treat his addiction, but lamented that his days are now oriented around the clinic. He had commuted 45 minutes from Bushwick to receive his methadone, a highly regulated opioid used to treat heroin and painkiller

JC Marin travels more than an hour to a methadone clinic in Brooklyn from his home in Copiague, Long Island, where his basement bears the remnants of his time working as a handyman.

dependence, as he does every day of the week. Sometimes he waits in line at the clinic for an hour for his turn. "You have to come every day. I hate it, I hate it, but you have to do it."

This is what opioid addiction recovery is like for more than 30,000 patients enrolled in New York City's approximately 70 methadone-based treatment programs, which provide medication-assisted treatment, counseling and other social services. Hundreds of thousands of patients across the country are enrolled in similar programs, which often receive government funding and are covered by Medicaid in New York.

For more than 40 years, methadone was the most effective method for people addicted to heroin to keep their cravings in check. But in 2002, the Food and Drug Administration approved another medication to treat opioid addiction: buprenorphine, sold most widely in a compound called Suboxone. Both methadone and buprenorphine are extremely effective in keeping recovering users from relapsing, according to medical research, but Suboxone is engineered to reduce the possibility of abuse and overdose. Crucially, the medication can be prescribed in doctors' offices and then taken at home.

Many hoped that buprenorphine could mean an end to the daily hurdles to receiving treatment for tens of thousands of patients: no additional commute, no security check, no waiting, no line for the plastic cup.

But today in the city, that is primarily true only for middle-class or upper-middle-class patients seeking help with their addiction.

More patients arrived at the clinic as Mr. Perez spoke. They were nearly all Hispanic or black. Those who are white, like Melissa Neilson, are often unemployed or have few resources to dedicate to recovery. She and her partner, JC Marin, visit the clinic from Copiague, Long Island, in a taxi paid for by Medicaid. More than two hours each way, six days a week, for their daily dose.

Methadone treatment was pioneered in New York, a city with a deep history of opioid addiction; access to the treatment is easier here than anywhere else in the United States.But because methadone is highly regulated — owing to fears that it could be sold in illegal markets — physicians can provide methadone for addiction treatment only in specialized clinics like Vincent Dole. Employment, child care, unexpected emergencies and other life events have to be oriented around the clinic. On the street, methadone is sometimes referred to as the "liquid handcuffs."

The limited data recently made available by the New York City health department hints at structural discrepancies in access to treatment that become obvious during visits to these clinics. In New York City, 53 percent of participants in methadone programs are Latino, 23 percent are black, and 21 percent are white, according to 2016 health department data.

The city said it does not keep track of the income or race of buprenorphine patients, and data on buprenorphine treatment demographics is sparse at the national level as well. A study published in 2016 in Drug and Alcohol Dependence, a scientific journal, found that

The Vincent Dole Clinic, which offers a methadone maintenance program, is in an unmarked building in an industrial section of Brooklyn near the Gowanus Expressway.

buprenorphine and methadone access were correlated with income and ethnicity in New York City. Without broad government surveys, precision is difficult; the report lamented that no nationally representative data on ethnicity or income has been published since 2006, when a survey by the Substance Abuse and Mental Health Services Administration showed that 92 percent of buprenorphine patients were white.

In 2016, according to data provided by the city, more than 13,600 New Yorkers filled prescriptions for Suboxone at least once — and nearly 80 percent paid for the medication with private insurance. No reliable payment data is available for methadone in New York City, but a representative for the Dole clinic said virtually all of its patients receive Medicaid.

City Hall has sought to increase the number of physicians certified to prescribe buprenorphine. Mayor Bill de Blasio and his wife, Chirlane McCray, have spoken about the urgent need to expand treatment options. But despite their efforts, the growth of buprenorphine pre-scribers has been slower than many experts would like.

"What this crisis is again calling attention to is the need for more health professionals to step in," said Dr. Hillary Kunins, an assistant commissioner at the New York City Department of Health. "I think because of stigma and because of inadequate education in health pro-fessional settings, physicians were not taught to think about addiction in their specialties."

Dr. Andrew Kolodny, an opioid addiction expert affiliated with Brandeis University, said regulatory burdens on buprenorphine by the government — like the eight-hour certification requirement — has likely discouraged physicians from offering it in their practices.

He added that many doctors who are certified to prescribe buprenorphine choose not to after realizing the complicated task of treating patients with substance abuse problems. Those who do work with the patients often do not accept insurance, he said, in some cases because demand is high and they can make more money charging directly. That means the patients must have enough money to pay out of pocket for the visit.

"Your insurance will pay for the prescription, but you have to pay for the doctor," he said.

What has emerged is a private and expensive market for buprenor-phine treatment.

The fight for equity in treatment for opioid addiction can feel like a multifront battle; in some cases, experts struggle just to persuade policymakers and nonspecialists that prescribing an opioid to a drug addict is a reasonable course of action. Numerous studies confirm that methadone and buprenorphine are both highly effective for treating opioid addiction. (The effectiveness of detoxification — total absti-nence from opioids — for long-term addiction management, which is strongly emphasized in popular treatment narratives, has been called into question by experts and by medical research. It can also leave those who relapse at higher risk for overdose.)

The clinics themselves are often vulnerable because they work with such a highly stigmatized population, especially in rapidly gentrifying areas. Mr. Perez was enrolled in the Cumberland Clinic on Flatbush Avenue, near the Barclays Center, before it closed late last year. Mount Sinai Beth Israel, which ran the clinic and also runs the Dole facility, had its lease for the clinic terminated when a private owner sold it to a development company. A new high-rise development is going up in its place.

Dr. Helena Hansen, a research psychiatrist and cultural anthropologist, said racially charged stereotypes historically associated with opioid and heroin addiction have led to persistent stigma around methadone. Methadone, she said, carries criminal connotations that can be traced back to the War on Drugs rhetoric that escalated in the 1960s.

Methadone clinics, Dr. Hansen pointed out, can often look and function like probation offices. "And they're organized as such," she said. "People line up, they have to have their urine checked, you have to come every day."

Noa Barreto, 43, started using heroin about four years ago after "a tragic loss" in his life. He was dealing drugs at the time and he "started getting high on my own supply." Two years ago, after battling with addiction, he made a decision to enroll in methadone treatment. Mr. Barreto said after he overcame the initial shock of entering treatment, he was able to reorient his day around the methadone doses.

"It's like a job, you know?" he said. "Once you get on it, and you become accustomed to it, it becomes easy. You get up in the morning and it becomes a routine."

Earlier this month, Mr. Barreto said, he had to turn down a job offer because it would interfere with his ability to get to the methadone clinic. Some patients who have made progress with their addiction are trusted with limited "take home" bottles, but the process can take months or years. And with good reason. When abused, methadone carries an extremely high potential for overdose. (Mr. Barreto currently qualifies for take-home bottles on the weekends; he visits the clinic five times a week.)

For Melissa Neilson and JC Marin, the car ride from Copiague, Long Island, to the methadone clinic in Brooklyn costs them time, but not money. It is covered by Medicaid.

Rick Harwood, the deputy director at the National Association of State Alcohol and Drug Abuse Directors, said the demographics of methadone clinics could be partly explained by patients who are middle class or white being less likely to see methadone as a treatment option.

"Ask people, middle class or otherwise, would they go to an opioid treatment program, a methadone clinic?" Mr. Harwood said. "Not too many of them probably would. A lot of times they're inconvenient to where they live, or are in depressed neighborhoods, places people might consider unsafe."

Mr. Harwood said that low-income patients could conceivably access buprenorphine treatment at methadone clinics, if they are interested. But methadone clinics are often already overwhelmed with methadone logistics and the social service programs they are required to provide; buprenorphine consultations are an additional service. That can produce an information gap in addition to a financial one.

Dr. Kolodny also said that, realistically, buprenorphine treatment cuts against the business interests of for-profit methadone clinics, which are becoming more common nationally.

Mr. Perez could be served well by the flexibility that Suboxone would give him as he manages employment as a tattoo artist. He said he would like to consider transitioning to buprenorphine treatment, but does not know where he can get it or how he might pay for it. Meanwhile, some long-term users, including Ms. Neilson, who travels to the clinic from Long Island, say that methadone has a more satisfying effect than buprenorphine.

"I tried to go back on Suboxone," she said. "I didn't feel sick, but I still wanted to get high. I had no energy not even to get up and take a shower, let alone leave the house or stand up." She added that she's afraid to transition away from methadone. "The sickness is not something I can describe to anybody. This is a better way to do it. Methadone. I'm never getting off."

Dr. Chinazo Cunningham, a Bronx-based addiction medicine expert who has worked with vulnerable populations for decades, said that she "just knew" a two-tier system would emerge, excluding many patients. But she stressed that methadone programs do important work for patients with complicated needs. Beyond drug treatment itself, the clinics provide a critical reprieve for patients without support networks.

"The people whose lives are a little bit more chaotic could benefit from methadone, or people who have poly-substance use, alcohol or cocaine, or others," said Dr. Cunningham, who is affiliated with Montefiore Medical Center, in the Bronx. "Primary-care settings have limited resources and maybe can't take on someone who is more complicated."

Such was the case with Jonathan Roman, 33. He is homeless and sleeps in his van. He arrived at the Vincent Dole clinic about eight months ago without insurance, looking for help with his addiction; the team at the clinic helped him enroll in Medicaid. They are also helping him find housing, he said, while speaking glowingly about his counselor at the clinic.

At one point, Mr. Roman estimated that he was using $300 of heroin a day, which he paid for by "stealing and doing side jobs." People took advantage of his addiction, he said, giving him work in construction and as an electrician but then paying him less than they should because they knew he was desperate. His dealer used to pick him up on payday, at 4:30 a.m., and drive him to the nearest A.T.M.

Mr. Roman said that for him and countless other patients, the concentrated resources available at the clinic provide a life-support system. He currently qualifies for take-home bottles of methadone, but he has refused them; the discipline of coming to the clinic each day helps him, he said.

"You can be on the good path, but if something happens in your life, and you think you're not worth anything, or that life is not worth living, you do stupid things," he said. "Now I think about all the things that I do and I laugh sometimes. I was this close to losing my life."

RYAN CHRISTOPHER JONES CONTRIBUTED REPORTING.

CHAPTER 4

Overprescription: Cause of the Crisis?

One question persists: What caused the crisis? A frequent culprit is the overprescription of opioids beginning in the late 1990s. A shift motivated partly by empathy for chronic pain and partly by profits became unmanageable as patients developed a tolerance for the powerful drugs. This chapter documents the many voices examining overprescription and the difficult shift to new medical protocols, which often exacerbated the crisis in the short term.

Tightening the Lid on Pain Prescriptions

BY BARRY MEIER | APRIL 8, 2012

SEATTLE — It was the type of conversation that Dr. Claire Trescott dreads: telling physicians that they are not cutting it.

But the large health care system here that Dr. Trescott helps manage has placed controls on how painkillers are prescribed, like making sure doctors do not prescribe too much. Doctors on staff have been told to abide by the guidelines or face the consequences.

So far, two doctors have decided to leave, and two more have remained but are being closely monitored.

"It is excruciating," said Dr. Trescott, who oversees primary care at Group Health. "These are often very good clinicians who just have this fatal flaw."

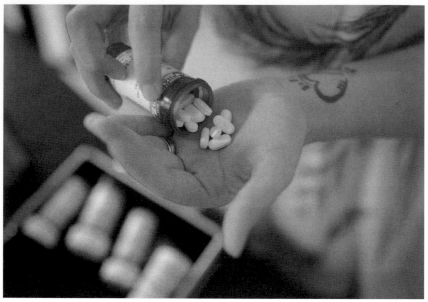

Hydrocodone is one of several medicines that Alisa Erkes takes for pain.

High-strength painkillers known as opioids represent the most widely prescribed class of medications in the United States. And over the last decade, the number of prescriptions for the strongest opioids has increased nearly fourfold, with only limited evidence of their long-term effectiveness or risks, federal data shows.

"Doctors are prescribing like crazy," said Dr. C. Richard Chapman, the director of the Pain Research Center at the University of Utah.

Medical professionals have long been on high alert about powerful painkillers like OxyContin because of their widespread abuse by teenagers and others for recreational purposes.

Now the alarm is extending from the street to an arena where the drugs had been considered legitimate and safe: doctors' offices where they are prescribed — and some say grossly overprescribed — for the treatment of long-term pain from back injuries, arthritis and other conditions.

Studies link narcotic painkillers to a variety of dangers, like sleep apnea, sharply reduced hormone production and, in the elderly, increased falls and hip fractures. The most extreme cases include fatal overdoses.

Data suggest that hundreds of thousands of patients nationwide may be on potentially dangerous dosages. And while no one questions that the medicines help countless patients and that most doctors prescribe them responsibly, there is a growing resistance to their creeping overuse. Experts say that doctors often simply keep patients on the drugs for years and that patients can develop a powerful psychological dependence on them that mirrors addiction.

But changing old habits can be difficult — for doctors and patients alike.

The most aggressive effort is under way here in Washington, where lawmakers last year imposed new requirements on doctors to refer patients taking high dosages of opioids — which include hydrocodone, fentanyl, methadone and oxycodone, the active ingredient in OxyContin — for evaluation by a pain specialist if their underlying condition is not improving.

Even before the new provisions took effect, some doctors stopped treating pain patients, and more have followed suit. Christine Link, 50, said that several doctors had refused to refill the prescription for painkillers she had taken for years for a degenerative joint disease.

"I am suffering, and I know I am not the only one," she said.

Washington State officials acknowledge some of the law's early deficiencies, including its sometimes indiscriminate application, and they are seeking to address them. But there is no retreat on the goal of moderating opioid use, and the movement extends well beyond Washington.

The federal Centers for Disease Control and Prevention has urged doctors to use opioids more judiciously, pointing to the easy availability of the drugs on the street and a mounting toll of overdose deaths; in 2008, the most recent year with available data, 14,800 people died in episodes involving prescription painkillers.

The Departments of Defense and Veterans Affairs are trying new programs to reduce use among active-duty troops and veterans.

"If I wake up, I wake up; if I die, I die." — Shawn Schneider, who was addicted to painkillers, on what went through his mind before he took 40 sleeping pills. He is now in treatment.

Various states are experimenting with restrictions, including Ohio, which is considering following the Washington model.

"We are trying to prepare our state for what we hope is the inevitable curbing of the use of opiates in chronic pain," said Orman Hall, the director of Ohio's Department of Alcohol and Drug Addiction Services.

The long-term use of opioids to treat chronic pain is relatively new. Until about 15 years ago, the drugs were largely reserved for postoperative, cancer or end-of-life care. But based on their success in those areas, pain experts argued the medications could be used to treat common kinds of long-term pain with little risk of addiction.

At the same time, pharmaceutical companies began to promote newer opioid formulations like OxyContin for chronic pain that could be used at greater strengths than traditional painkillers. Sales of painkillers reached about $8.5 billion last year, compared with $4.4 billion in 2001, according to the consulting firm IMS Health.

Along with Purdue Pharma, the maker of OxyContin, other producers include Johnson & Johnson and Endo Pharmaceuticals.

Dr. Russell K. Portenoy, who championed the drugs' broader use, said the new data about the potential high-dose risks was concerning. But he added that the medications were extremely valuable and that their benefits needed to be factored into policies like the one in Washington State.

"I don't think opioids need to be thought of any differently than any other therapies," said Dr. Portenoy, chairman of the pain medicine and palliative care department at Beth Israel Medical Center in New York. "It is just that right now, they have got our attention."

A pain expert here in Seattle, Dr. Jane C. Ballantyne, said she once agreed with Dr. Portenoy, but she now finds herself in the role of former believer turned crusading reformer.

"We started on this whole thing because we were on a mission to help people in pain," she said of the medical profession's embrace of opioids. "But the long-term outcomes for many of these patients are appalling, and it is ending up destroying their lives."

ALARMS SOUNDED

The clues were buried in the dullest of places: thousands of workers' compensation claims.

In 2006, a state official here, Dr. Gary Franklin, called together 15 medical experts to discuss some troubling data found in the records.

Thirty-two injured workers who were prescribed opioids for pain had died of overdoses involving the drugs. In addition, in just a few years, the strength of the average daily dose of the most powerful opioids prescribed to patients treated through the workers' compensation program had shot up by more than 50 percent. The number of patients taking the drugs in large quantities had grown to 10,000.

Doctors often increase opioid dosages because patients can adjust, or develop tolerance, to the drugs and need greater amounts to get the same effect. Pain specialists, including Dr. Portenoy of Beth Israel, had argued that it was safe to increase dosages so long as doctors made sure that patients were improving.

But the Washington data suggested that doctors were not monitoring patients; they were simply prescribing more and more. Such practices are common, said Dr. Trescott, the official at Group Health in Seattle, because treating pain patients, who are often also depressed or anxious, is time-consuming and difficult.

"Doctors end up chasing pain" instead of focusing on treating the underlying condition, she said.

That is what happened several years ago to a former nurse, Mary Crossman, after she was found to have lupus, an autoimmune disease that can cause severe joint and muscle pain. Her doctor put her on Oxy-Contin and methadone and then raised the dosage every six months or so after she developed tolerance to the lower dosage.

Five years later, she was taking dosages so high that another doctor who examined her was shocked. "She said, 'I don't want you to die,' " Mrs. Crossman recalled.

In 2007, the Washington State panel approved a guideline that urged doctors to refer patients on large dosages for evaluation if they were not improving. Two professional groups representing pain specialists had already taken a similar step. But the Washington action had an important difference that soon proved contentious: it set a dosage level meant to prompt the referral.

As with most medical guidelines, doctors in Washington largely ignored the panel's suggestions, a later survey found — until last year, when the guidelines became law.

That bill moved so quickly through the State Legislature that its opponents were caught off guard. The maker of OxyContin, Purdue Pharma, tried and failed to stop it. Several national pain experts, including some with ties to the drug industry, also sought to block it, saying the new provisions would cause chaos by restricting patient access to care.

Even some supporters of the new law agreed that there was little evidence to support the dosage threshold, which was the amount of any opioid equivalent in strength to a daily dose of 120 milligrams of morphine. Nonetheless, they believed that drastic change was needed.

"I thought the new law was a necessary evil," said one Seattle-area physician, Dr. Charles Chabal.

A CYCLE OF ABUSE

The state law has transformed the clinic at the University of Washington into a pain treatment center of last resort — and Dr. Ballantyne, the pain expert, into an appeals judge of sorts because she sees patients referred for evaluation under the law. On a recent day, she was seeing a stream of castoff patients, including Ms. Link, who sat hunched in a wheelchair, suffering from a degenerative joint disease.

"They all said that I can't treat you, you need to see a specialist," Ms. Link said of her other doctors.

Before the widespread use of opioids, the University of Washington's medical school was known for an approach to chronic pain that emphasized nondrug treatments like physical therapy and counseling. Some specialists like Dr. Ballantyne, who moved here a year ago, are now determined to revive that tradition.

"If doctors understood how hard it is to get patients off of these drugs, they would not prescribe them to begin with," she said.

Born and educated in England, Dr. Ballantyne was in charge of pain treatment for more than a decade at Massachusetts General Hospital in Boston before taking a post in 2008 at the University of Pennsylvania, in Philadelphia. She and her husband, who is also a doctor, bought an old house there to renovate, but when the University of Washington called, she jumped.

Dr. Ballantyne, 63, once embraced the wider use of opioids. Her transition to skepticism began about a decade ago, when she noticed that hospitalized patients taking high dosages screamed when they were examined — as if the drugs had increased their sensitivity to pain.

She decided to research long-term data about the drugs and published a medical journal article in 2003 with her findings. It concluded that high doses might not be safe or effective.

Other experts accused her of undercutting years of effort to erase stigmas about the drugs. "They'd say, 'How could you do something like this after all we have worked for?' " Dr. Ballantyne recalled.

Since then, other researchers have published papers about the drugs' medical dangers. Studies have shown, for example, that the drugs greatly suppress the production of sexual hormones.

"It is not just our sex lives that go away; it is our ability to get things done," said Dr. Chapman, of the University of Utah.

Dr. Portenoy, the expert in New York, agreed that doctors needed to be aware of such risks. But he said that the dosage threshold used by Washington officials was arbitrary and that the state had failed to put a system in place to evaluate the law's impact on patients.

"You would always want to look at outcomes to see what you did either harmed or helped," said Dr. Portenoy, who consults with opioid producers.

A patient advocacy group, the American Pain Foundation, which receives much of its financing from drug makers, has continued to oppose the law, calling it "inhumane." And even some supporters believe it needs reworking.

Dr. Ballantyne said she also feared that the problems encountered by patients seeking treatment could cause an adverse reaction to the law. But she said she hoped that the quandary for patients like Ms. Link, who was given a new painkiller prescription, were "teething pains" that would be remedied.

She has little patience, however, for those who believe that the opioid problem can be solved simply by screening out those patients who might abuse the drugs.

"I think that after 20 years of a failed experiment that there are not many people supporting this except for the die-hards and the pharmaceutical industry," she said.

A LOST GENERATION

About a year ago, Mary Crossman, the former nurse with lupus, was at a neighborhood cookout with her husband when she noticed something odd: she was more relaxed, talkative and sociable than she had been in a long while.

Not long before, her doctor had suggested reducing her use of the painkillers OxyContin and methadone. The doctor, who worked at Group Health, said they would reduce the drugs slowly but warned Mrs. Crossman that she would initially feel more pain and increased anxiety.

Mrs. Crossman, who is 58, was scared but agreed to try. When her lupus flared up, she took more drugs, but over all, her daily dosages steadily came down. Today, she no longer takes methadone, and the amount of OxyContin she takes each day is 80 percent lower than it was a year ago.

Looking back, she said the high dosages helped mask her pain. But the pain relief came at a price; she now feels more mentally alert.

"There are days when I still hurt a lot, but over all I'm doing O.K.," she said.

Big health care systems like Group Health, which treats 420,000 patients at 25 clinics throughout Washington, can oversee how doctors prescribe drugs and provide patients with alternative treatments. Over the last four years, Group Health has cut the percentage of patients on high opioid dosages in half, the system says, and reduced the average daily dose among patients who regularly take opioids by one-third.

The system is now examining how those changes have affected patients. Studies elsewhere suggest the benefits of lower opioid use may be significant for many patients. For example, Danish researchers have published a study indicating that chronic pain patients getting nondrug treatments recover at a rate four times as high as those on opioids.

"These drugs don't seem to be even doing what they are supposed," said Dr. Per Sjogren, a pain expert in Copenhagen who led the study.

The obstacles to lower opioid use remain formidable, however; both insurers and public agencies must be willing to pay for other treatments, which can be costly.

"You can't just take things away," said Dr. Roger Chou, an associate professor at Oregon Health and Science University in Portland. "You have to give patients alternatives."

There is also political and professional resistance to adapting requirements like those at Group Health to taxpayer-financed programs like Medicaid.

The Food and Drug Administration indicated in 2008 that it might require that doctors receive several hours of mandatory training in the use of opioids as a condition of prescribing them. But in 2010, the agency backed away from that stance in the face of opposition from some medical and patient advocacy groups. In addition, although the Obama administration announced plans last year to introduce legislation containing such a mandate, it has yet to do so.

Few programs are in place to deal with patients now on high opioid dosages who are not benefiting from them.

If the patients were taken off the medications, many would experience severe withdrawal or have to take addiction treatment drugs for years. Even avid believers in the new direction, like Dr. Ballantyne, suggest that it might be necessary to keep those patients on the opioids and to focus instead on preventing new pain patients from getting caught in the cycle.

"I think we are dealing with a lost generation of patients," she said.

How Doctors Helped Drive the Addiction Crisis

BY RICHARD FRIEDMAN | NOV. 7, 2015

THERE HAS BEEN an alarming and steady increase in the mortality rate of middle-aged white Americans since 1999, according to a study published last week. This increase — half a percent annually — contrasts starkly with decreasing death rates in all other age and ethnic groups and with middle-aged people in other developed countries.

So what is killing middle-aged white Americans? Much of the excess death is attributable to suicide and drug and alcohol poisonings. Opioid painkillers like OxyContin prescribed by physicians contribute significantly to these drug overdoses.

Thus, it seems that an opioid overdose epidemic is at the heart of this rise in white middle-age mortality. The rate of death from prescription opioids in the United States increased more than fourfold between 1999 and 2010, dwarfing the combined mortality from heroin and cocaine. In 2013 alone, opioids were involved in 37 percent of all fatal drug overdoses.

Driving this opioid epidemic, in large part, is a disturbing change in the attitude within the medical profession about the use of these drugs to treat pain. Traditionally, opioid analgesics were largely used to treat pain stemming from terminal diseases like cancer, or for short-term uses, such as recovering from surgery.

But starting in the 1990s, there has been a vast expansion in the long-term use of opioid painkillers to treat chronic nonmalignant medical conditions, like low-back pain, sciatica and various musculoskeletal problems. To no small degree, this change in clinical practice was encouraged through aggressive marketing by drug companies that made new and powerful opioids, like OxyContin, an extended-release form of oxycodone that was approved for use in 1995.

The pitch to doctors seemed sensible and seductive: Be proactive with pain and treat it aggressively. After all, doctors have frequently been accused of being insensitive to pain or undertreating it. Here was the corrective, and who in their right mind would argue that physicians shouldn't try to relieve pain whenever possible?

Well, doctors clearly got the message: The medical use of these drugs grew tenfold in just 20 years. Nearly half of all prescriptions by pain specialists are for opioids. But strikingly, primary care physicians, who generally do not have any particular expertise or training in pain management, prescribed far more opioids overall than pain specialists. For example, in 2012, 18 percent of all prescriptions for opioid analgesics were written by family practitioners, and 15 percent by internists, compared to 5 percent for pain specialists. (This partly reflects the fact that there are fewer pain specialists than primary care doctors.)

The consequences of this epidemic have been staggering. Opioids are reported in 39 percent of all emergency room visits for nonmedical drug use. They are highly addictive and can produce significant depressive and anxiety states. And the annual direct health care costs of opioid users has been estimated to be more than eight times that of nonusers.

But most surprising — and disturbing — of all is that there is actually very weak evidence that opioids are safe or effective for the long-term treatment of nonmalignant pain. So how did they become so popular for these uses? A large review article conducted between 1983 and 2012 found that only 25 of these were randomized controlled trials and only one study lasted three months or longer. The review concluded that there was little good evidence to support the safety or efficacy of long-term opioid therapy for nonmalignant pain. (In contrast, there is little question that opioid analgesics are highly effective for the relief of short-term pain.)

Furthermore, a large 2006 Danish study of a nationally representative sample of 10,066 people that compared opioid and nonopioid users found that opioid use was significantly associated with the reporting of severe pain, poor health, unemployment, and greater use of the health care system. It appears that long-term opioid use did not significantly relieve pain or improve quality of life in this well-designed study.

Worse, there is a well-known syndrome of opioid-induced hyperalgesia in which opioids, paradoxically, can actually increase a person's sensitivity to painful stimuli.

What the public — and physicians — should know is that there is strong evidence that nonsteroidal anti-inflammatory drugs (Nsaids), like Motrin, and other analgesics like Tylenol are actually safer and more effective for many painful conditions than opioid painkillers.

For example, one study found that a combination of Motrin and Tylenol had a much lower so-called number needed to treat than opioids. (The number needed to treat represents the number of people who must be treated for one person to benefit.) A lower number indicates a more effective treatment.

So how should we deal with the national crisis of opioid misuse, addiction and overdose? The Food and Drug Administration has already taken some tiny, though inadequate, steps forward in recent years by issuing a Risk Evaluation and Mitigation Strategy in 2012 that requires the makers of opioids to provide doctors with training and education about using them safely, and adding warnings to drug labels.

What is really needed is a sea change within the medical profession itself. We should be educating and training our medical students and residents about the risks and limited benefits of opioids in treating pain. All medical professional organizations should back mandated education about safe opioid treatment as a prerequisite for licensure and prescribing. At present, the American Academy of Family Physicians opposes such a measure because it could limit patient access to pain treatment with opioids, which I think is misguided. Don't we want family doctors, who are significant prescribers of opioids, to learn about their limitations and dangers?

It is physicians who, in large part, unleashed the current opioid epidemic with their promiscuous use of these drugs; we have a large responsibility to end it.

RICHARD A. FRIEDMAN IS A PROFESSOR OF CLINICAL PSYCHIATRY AND THE DIRECTOR OF THE PSYCHOPHARMACOLOGY CLINIC AT THE WEILL CORNELL MEDICAL COLLEGE, AND A CONTRIBUTING OPINION WRITER.

Doctors Will Play a Critical Role in the Opioid Epidemic

OPINION | BY THE NEW YORK TIMES | AUG. 30, 2016

ABOUT HALF of opioid overdose deaths involve prescription drugs. With that stark fact in mind, the surgeon general, Dr. Vivek Murthy, sent an unusually direct plea last week to 2.3 million doctors and other health care workers to help fight the opioid epidemic by treating pain "safely and effectively." A website for his "Turn the Tide" campaign highlights alternative, nonaddictive treatments for pain. Not only doctors but also policy makers, insurance companies and other players in the health care system should pay attention.

Prescriptions for opioids such as oxycodone and methadone have quadrupled since 1999, as have opioid overdose deaths — more than 28,000 in 2014, up 14 percent from the year before. While prescriptions for opioids peaked in 2012, their use remains high by historical standards. And many people who were prescribed opioids have gone on to use illegal opioids like heroin and fentanyl.

For cancer patients or people near the end of their lives, opioids are often the only effective medicine. But doctors have many more options for treating back pain, migraines and pain related to surgery — physical therapy, anti-inflammatory drugs, acupuncture, exercise and so on. Some doctors overlook these alternatives because opioids are easy to prescribe or because patients demand them.

A further problem is that some insurance plans do not cover alternative treatments like physical therapy and acupuncture, or they impose so many limits and high co-pays on them that in many cases both doctors and patients find opioids a less expensive option. In some rural areas, the nearest physical therapist may be many miles away.

One fix here seems obvious: Federal and state lawmakers can require insurers to cover these services, a cheaper option over the long term than addiction treatment. And they should also find ways to expand access to health services by subsidizing doctors, therapists and other health care workers to make periodic visits to remote areas.

Even when opioids are necessary, doctors can minimize the risk of addiction by taking a few precautions. They can write prescriptions for low doses and relatively short time periods. They should pay attention to monitoring programs that most states have set up to make sure a person is not getting multiple prescriptions from different doctors. And doctors can steer to treatment patients who are obviously addicted.

Doctors are not the only ones responsible for the opioid epidemic, but as Dr. Murthy makes clear, they'll have to play a leading role in the fight against it.

With Overdoses on Rise, Cities and Counties Look for Someone to Blame

BY MITCH SMITH AND MONICA DAVEY | DEC. 20, 2017

AKRON, OHIO — Citing a spike in overdose deaths, growing demands for drug treatment and a strained budget, officials here in Summit County filed a lawsuit late Wednesday against companies that make or distribute prescription opioids. On Monday, Smith County in Tennessee did the same. And on Tuesday, nine cities and counties in Michigan announced similar suits.

Cities, counties and states across the country are turning to the courts in the spiraling opioid crisis. What began a few years ago with a handful of lawsuits has grown into a flood of claims that drug companies improperly marketed opioids or failed to report suspiciously large orders. Close to 200 civil cases have been filed by local governments in the federal courts; dozens of other suits are playing out in state courts; and attorneys general from 41 states have banded together to explore legal options.

"There's a new case being filed virtually every day, and I don't see any end in sight," said Paul J. Hanly Jr., a lawyer who represents some of the local governments.

Scores of plaintiffs' lawyers met in Cleveland this week, where a judge has been assigned to oversee at least 189 of the federal cases — an indication, some lawyers say, that the legal fight could start to move more quickly and that its disparate strands might be worked out in one place. Some lawyers liken the situation to the state litigation against the tobacco industry in the 1990s, which ended with a global settlement, and involved some of the same lawyers.

"This litigation is like a big hammer — it's like a tool where you're hitting somebody upside the head to get their attention," said Mike

Moore, who as Mississippi attorney general filed the first state case against the tobacco industry in the 1990s and who now represents some government entities. "We have a public health emergency. It's time to quit talking about it and, if people are serious about fixing it, let's sit down and resolve it."

Representatives for some of the drug makers and distributors deny the claims in the lawsuits and say they intend to vigorously defend their companies. In written statements, several companies pointed to efforts that they and industry groups have taken to stem opioid abuses and noted the role of the federal authorities, including the Food and Drug Administration, in overseeing their products. They also rejected comparisons to tobacco.

"Unlike the past tobacco litigation, our medicines are approved by F.D.A., prescribed by doctors, and dispensed by pharmacists, as treatments for patients suffering from severe pain," Robert Josephson, a spokesman for Purdue Pharma, which developed OxyContin, said in a written response to questions.

Here in Akron, officials said legally prescribed painkillers were often a precursor to addiction, overdose and drug abuse. Nanette Kelly, an Akron resident, said she became hooked on prescription pain pills after a back injury years ago and eventually turned to heroin.

"It's hard to stay straight and be good," said Ms. Kelly, who is undergoing treatment, "because there's just heroin everywhere."

Matthew J. Maletta, executive vice president and chief legal officer at the drug company Endo, said a comprehensive solution "must not only consider the product supply chain, but also individual patient risk factors and the role of prescribing health care providers." Criminal trafficking of the drugs, including illegal internet sales and importation, also must be addressed, he said.

The legal battle is playing out as the sale of prescription opioids, which include oxycodone and hydrocodone, have quadrupled since 1999, as have overdose deaths. More than 183,000 people died from overdoses tied to prescription opioids in the 15 years leading up to

2015. Life expectancy in the United States dropped for the second year in a row in 2016, federal officials reported this week, largely driven by drug overdoses, the vast majority of which were opioid-related. And the larger drug crisis, including heroin and fentanyl obtained illicitly, is swamping the resources of local governments and draining their budgets, officials say.

Summit County officials say they spent $66 million dealing with the crisis between 2012 and last year. The county's child protective agency spent more than $21 million in that period relocating children from homes where a relative was using opioids. Akron firefighters average around 100 overdose responses each month. And a mobile morgue was brought in when the medical examiner ran out of room.

"We've had enough here," said Ilene Shapiro, the county executive, who has declared a public health emergency. She said she hoped the courts could force changes in the way the drugs are marketed and, perhaps, impose a hefty financial settlement or judgment.

In Barberton, a small city in Summit County that is also suing, rookie police officers must quickly master how to make death notifications, how to refer addicts to treatment and how to administer Narcan, the overdose antidote. The police chief, Vince Morber, said the pharmaceutical companies "owe us an apology."

"They absolutely knew what they were doing: Their business practices, the way they did it, the way they marketed it," said Chief Morber.

But legal experts said the lawsuits against the drug makers and distributors are anything but simple. The cases vary when it comes to the companies they name as defendants and are complicated by all sorts of elements — including the roles of others in what has happened, from medical doctors to heroin dealers to the F.D.A., which regulates prescription medications.

"My guess is that nobody wants to really try these cases," said Richard C. Ausness, a professor at the University of Kentucky College of Law.

Critics say the litigation is a sideshow in the opioid debate — a chance for lawyers to make money and politicians to make headlines —

rather than a lasting solution in the overwhelming crisis, which the president's Council of Economic Advisers last month estimated as having cost $504 billion in 2015.

"Indeed, by allowing them to take credit for doing something about the problem, the lawsuits may take the pressure off of public officials" to make real changes, Lars Noah, a professor at the University of Florida College of Law, said.

But lawyers for some counties, cities and states say the litigation could force real changes, such as far wider availability of overdose antidotes, sufficient money to get all addicts into treatment, and the development of a robust prevention and education program. The consolidation of the federal cases in a so-called multidistrict litigation could also speed the process, the lawyers said.

"It's a major opportunity to have a significant impact on this health epidemic now and not five years from now," said Joseph F. Rice, whose firm, Motley Rice, represents some of the cases, and who played a central role in negotiating the tobacco settlement. "Will the parties take advantage? Will the court take advantage? That's yet to be seen."

In Summit County, the number of fatal drug overdoses has subsided slightly since a peak of 298 last year, but paramedics, politicians and law enforcement officials still view opioids as an uncontained epidemic with no easy fixes.

Firefighters say they sometimes revive the same person again and again, and the medical examiner has gotten used to notifying families of drug deaths of multiple relatives. One woman lost two siblings and two nephews to overdoses in less than a year. Charlene Maxen and her husband, Jim, lost their two sons to opioid overdoses in the same month in 2015.

"I used to look at people that never had a family and say, 'What do they do when they get old?' " said Mr. Maxen, a retired accountant. "We're going to find out."

Dan Horrigan, the mayor of Akron, said the crisis had become "a gut punch to the community, and we need to be able to get a handle on it." He said a number of ground-level efforts to help addicts here showed promise, but "there is a fire going on and it needs more water to put it out."

Among the signs for hope: A health clinic that opens before dawn and provides methadone for people seeking to end their opioid addictions; home visits by city workers offering help to people who recently overdosed; and Judge Joy Malek Oldfield's drug court, where a stream of young defendants approached the bench on Monday to receive praise, scoldings and even applause.

"When you get sober, it's not just rainbows and unicorns," the judge told one. "But it's a better life, don't you think?"

Judge Oldfield said about 90 percent of people in drug court were addicted to opiates, which she called "much more difficult to manage" than other addictions. One man, shackled and clad in an orange jail jumpsuit, appeared in front of her again on Monday. He had relapsed not long ago.

"I'm glad you're alive," Judge Oldfield told him.

MITCH SMITH REPORTED FROM AKRON, AND MONICA DAVEY FROM CHICAGO.

CHAPTER 5

The Response by Government and Law Enforcement

Government responses to the opioid epidemic have been conflicted. Affected states have led the way with new approaches to the disease of addiction, shifting resources to expanded addiction treatment and increased availability of anti-overdose drugs. This shift has been aided by sympathetic police departments and families affected by drug abuse calling for a compassionate response to addiction. However, longstanding stigma around addiction remains at all levels of government, and resurfaces in Trump administration priorities — tough prosecutions for drug dealers and minimal support for recovery treatment.

In Annual Speech, Vermont Governor Shifts Focus to Drug Abuse

BY KATHARINE Q. SEELYE | JAN. 8, 2014

MONTPELIER, VT. — In a sign of how drastic the epidemic of drug addiction here has become, Gov. Peter Shumlin on Wednesday devoted his entire State of the State Message to what he said was "a full-blown heroin crisis" gripping Vermont.

"In every corner of our state, heroin and opiate drug addiction threatens us," he said. He said he wanted to reframe the public debate to encourage officials to respond to addiction as a chronic disease, with treatment and support, rather than with only punishment and incarceration.

"The time has come for us to stop quietly averting our eyes from the growing heroin addiction in our front yards," Governor Shumlin said, "while we fear and fight treatment facilities in our backyards."

Last year, he said, nearly twice as many people here died from heroin overdoses as the year before. Since 2000, Vermont has seen an increase of more than 770 percent in treatment for opiate addictions, up to 4,300 people in 2012.

Governor Shumlin, a Democrat now in his second term, used his State of the State Message last year to focus almost entirely on education. This year, he appears to be one of the first, if not the only, governor to use his message, all 34 minutes of it, to focus exclusively on drug addiction and detail its costs, in dollars and lives.

Such speeches mark the opening of a legislative session and traditionally feature some pomp and back-patting as governors lay out their broad agendas for the year to come. Here, the mood in the packed House chamber of the Statehouse was somber as lawmakers considered the scope of the drug problem.

While it may be acute in Vermont, it is not isolated. In the past few years, officials have reported a surge in the use of heroin in New England, with a sharp rise in overdoses and deaths, as well as robberies and other crimes common among addicts. Those same statistics are being replicated across the country. Lawmakers in virtually every state are introducing legislation in response to what is rapidly being perceived as a public health crisis.

"The Centers for Disease Control and most national experts agree there's an epidemic of drug overdose deaths in America," Dr. Harry L. Chen, Vermont's health commissioner, said in an interview. He said the rate of overdose deaths across the country had tripled since 1990.

"Nationwide, more people die of drug overdoses than from motor vehicle crashes," he said.

Gov. Peter Shumlin, a Democrat, used his State of the State Message on Wednesday in Montpelier to encourage public debate on the growing problem of drug abuse and addiction in his state.

Dr. Chen said the highest rates of substance abuse were found in New England and the Northeast. No one really knows why, he said, except that the region is a wide-open market for dealers with easy access from New York, Boston and Philadelphia. Law enforcement can be spotty in the rural areas up here, and users are willing to pay top prices.

A $6 bag of heroin in New York City fetches $10 in southern New England and up to $30 or $40 in northern New England, law enforcement officials said. The dealer gets a tremendous profit margin, while the addict pays half of what he might have to pay for prescription painkillers, which have become harder to obtain.

Democrats, who control both houses of the Legislature, lauded the governor's single-minded focus.

"He hit it absolutely right," said Senator Richard Sears, chairman of the Judiciary Committee. "I've been dealing with addicted folks for years and have seen the increase in crime related to this addiction problem."

Republicans were not impressed, saying that Governor Shumlin should have made room for other big issues confronting the state, especially problems with the rollout of its health care exchange.

"We do have to tackle addiction, but people day after day are asking me about health care," said Representative Heidi Scheuermann, a Republican from Stowe.

She said that the governor's proposal for what would be the nation's first single-payer health insurance plan had also caused considerable confusion and controversy and that the speech was both "a missed opportunity" to address it and "a way to change the subject."

Regardless, the picture Mr. Shumlin painted was grim. Every week, he said, more than $2 million worth of heroin and other opiates are trafficked into Vermont. And nearly 80 percent of inmates in the state are jailed on drug-related charges.

The governor made a plea for more money for treatment programs, noting that incarcerating a person for a week costs the state $1,120, while a week of treatment at a state-financed center costs $123. He asked for money to expand treatment centers, where more than 500 addicts are on waiting lists. He also called for rapid intervention programs so that addicts could be directed to treatment as soon as they see the blue lights flashing from police cars — supposedly the moment when they are most likely to accept help. To discourage high-volume dealers from coming into the state, he is seeking tougher laws.

During his speech, Mr. Shumlin singled out specially invited guests. They included Bess O'Brien, director of "The Hungry Heart," a documentary about drug addiction in Vermont; Dustin Machia, a recovering addict who appeared in the movie and stole more than $20,000 worth of farm equipment from his parents to support his habit; and Dr. Fred Holmes, Mr. Machia's physician. They sat in the chamber's balcony and drew standing ovations.

Mr. Shumlin also wants to encourage discussions on ways to prevent addiction in the first place. He is providing a grant for an entourage from "The Hungry Heart" to visit every high school in the state.

The group will include Skip Gates of Skowhegan, Me., whose son Will, a science major at the University of Vermont and a ski racer, died of a heroin overdose in 2009. "I never knew any human being could feel this much pain," Mr. Gates says in the movie of his son's death. "It has redefined the rest of my life."

A Call to Arms on a Vermont Heroin Epidemic

BY KATHARINE Q. SEELYE | FEB. 27, 2014

RUTLAND, VT. — Block by block, this city in central Vermont has been fighting a heroin epidemic so entrenched that it has confounded all efforts to combat it.

On Cottage Street, the foot traffic is heavy in and out of No. 24 ½, a red two-story cottage set back from the street, where visitors stay less than a minute.

"We know what they're doing in there," Victoria DeLong, a longtime neighbor, said of the house, which the police say is owned by an absentee landlord and is a haven for drug dealers. "It's like shopping at the Grand Union," Ms. DeLong said. "In and out, in and out."

Long visible at the street level in towns and cities across the country, the extent of the opiate scourge in rural Vermont burst into the national consciousness last month, when Gov. Peter Shumlin devoted his entire State of the State message to what he said was a "full-blown heroin crisis." Much of New England is now also reporting record overdoses and deaths.

For some communities just starting to reckon with drugs, Mr. Shumlin's words were a call to arms; for Rutland, they offered a sense of solidarity as this city of 17,000 moves ahead with efforts to help reclaim its neighborhoods and its young people, not to mention its reputation.

Rutland is a blue-collar town that rose to prominence in the mid-1800s with the excavation of nearby marble quarries and the arrival of the railroad. It stepped up its fight against heroin more than a year ago much the way addicts do when they try to stop using — by finally admitting the problem.

"There's probably not a person in Rutland County whose life has not been affected by opiate addiction in one way or another," said Jeffrey D. McKee, director of psychiatric services at the Rutland Regional Medical Center.

Victoria DeLong of Rutland, Vt., pointing out a house where drug dealing occurs. "We know what they're doing in there," she said.

Since acknowledging the problem, the police have come to view addiction as a disease, not just a law enforcement issue, and have joined with social service providers to take a more data-driven, coordinted approach to homes with multiple problems. City agencies and residents have joined forces to revitalize their neighborhoods and eliminate blight.

Mr. Shumlin, a Democrat, has directed money to Rutland to help put in place a rapid intervention program to divert certain drug abusers into treatment instead of jail; if they complete the treatment, they will not be prosecuted, giving them a better chance of finding a job.

And the city has opened its first methadone clinic. Residents had opposed one for years, but the need became too acute. Now, those needing this form of treatment do not have to travel an hour away; the clinic, which opened in November, expects to serve 400 people by the end of the year.

One of the galvanizing events occurred in September 2012, when a man was inhaling gas from an aerosol can while driving on city streets. The police say he passed out with his foot on the accelerator and plowed into a bank of parked cars at 80 miles an hour, killing Carly Ferro, 17, a high school student who was leaving work.

It was a sign to many that the city had spun out of control. Rutland was still mired in the recession, burglaries were up and residents had little confidence in city institutions. The Police Department, for example, faced allegations of officer misconduct, including watching pornography at work.

And drugs were everywhere.

"I was shocked at the depth of addiction here," said James W. Baker, a former director of the Vermont State Police, who was brought in as police chief in 2012 to overhaul the department. "We had open drug markets going on in the street."

And residents began to feel that the relaxed quality of life they cherished in Vermont was eroding.

"More and more people's homes were being broken into, and that raised the alarm," said Korrine Rodrigue, a public health researcher here.

It became clear that the city could not arrest its way out of addiction and that the police alone could not handle the multiple issues that were arising from drug abuse. And so the police began meeting with social workers, advocates for victims of domestic violence and child abuse, building inspectors and others.

"You can't separate child abuse, domestic violence and opiate abuse because in many situations, it all resides in the same house," Chief Baker said. "Now we'll set up an intervention, not just wait for something to happen."

They began mapping service calls to detect patterns. This led to the identification of a 10-block target zone in the city's Northwest sector as its most critical "hot spot." It receives 73 percent of all police calls, Ms. Rodrigue said, and 80 percent of burglaries.

Rutland, Vt., a city of 17,000, is trying to restore its young people and its reputation.

In this zone, troubled houses are interspersed with those that are better kept.

During a stroll last week in the neighborhood, Sherri Durgin-Campbell, a volunteer community mediator who owns a well-tended Victorian, pointed out drug houses and also stately homes, including one for sale with a wraparound porch and fancy kitchen.

"That guy's house has been on the market for over a year," she said. "He was originally asking $300,000 but he would gladly take $99,000."

The next day, the police conducted a drug raid on a nearby house, and a few hours later it went up in flames; investigators said the cause was arson but they have not determined the motive.

Many believe that part of the drug problem lies in the high conversion rate of single-family homes into multiunit rentals. The police say such units can be breeding grounds for drugs because of a well-established network, mostly of young women, who live in them and play host to out-of-town dealers. The dealers can make quick money by buying heroin in New York or Springfield, Mass., for as little as $6 a bag and selling it here for $30. About $2 million in heroin is trafficked every week in Vermont.

"If you're a guy from New York, you can come here with 500 bags of heroin, sell it and sleep with three different women before you go home the next day," said Chief Baker. Many of the women, he said, receive rent subsidies and food stamps and use heroin themselves. "The entire infrastructure is here for these guys to function, make quick money and leave," he said.

To help focus more attention on the drug problem, Rutland applied a year ago for a $1 million federal grant from the Department of Justice, which it did not get. But it used the application as a blueprint to organize a communitywide coalition of concerned citizens and government agencies. It calls itself Project Vision and it complements the work of the police and social services.

The project's overarching goals are to revitalize the 10-block target area, strengthen neighborhoods and reduce substance abuse. One of its first steps was to hold a block party last fall near where Ms. Ferro was killed.

"The point was to say, 'This is our community and we're taking it back,' " said Joseph Kraus, a former utility executive who is chairman of Project Vision.

Last week, after months of preliminary work, its members laid out specific goals. The police want to cut residential burglaries in half by the end of the year. Project Vision intends to reduce the number of blighted homes in the target zone to 15 from 21 by rehabilitating or razing six of them.

Two-thirds of the homes in the target area are multiunit apartments; Project Vision hopes to reduce that number to 50 percent within three years by buying back properties, perhaps having nonprofit groups restore them and resell them to owners who would live in them.

The frenzy of activity has inspired people like Linda Justin to do outreach on their own. Moved by what she said were "deteriorating" conditions, Ms. Justin, 65, has wound down her real estate business, cashed in her 401(k) and "adopted" a square city block, where she has been meeting residents every Sunday and "building relationships." She offers to help clean up houses and was preparing recently to connect a young heroin addict she had met with the proper agencies for treatment.

Mayor Christopher Louras has been going door to door with work crews as they install brighter streetlights.

"A byproduct of that outreach is to talk to neighbors and let them know that we're interested in their quality of life and giving them a greater sense of security," said the mayor, whose own nephew was arrested in 2012 on drug-related charges.

These efforts are in their earliest stages, but burglaries and thefts in Rutland were already down slightly in 2013 from 2012, according to police figures, although drug offenses — and overdoses — were up.

Anecdotally, some business owners said they had seen little change, so far.

Paul Ross, for one, who owns Ramunto's Pizza Shop, said he still sees drug deals "right in my parking lot." And some residents of the target area resent that so many people from outside the zone are making decisions for their neighborhood.

Mr. Kraus, the Project Vision chairman, said the project was "a work in progress," but he was positive about Rutland's future.

"Nobody's proud that we find ourselves in this circumstance," he said. "But we confront our problems and deal with them." He vowed improvements by this time next year.

In Heroin Crisis, White Families Seek Gentler War on Drugs

BY KATHARINE Q. SEELYE | OCT. 30, 2015

NEWTON, N.H. — When Courtney Griffin was using heroin, she lied, disappeared, and stole from her parents to support her $400-a-day habit. Her family paid her debts, never filed a police report and kept her addiction secret — until she was found dead last year of an overdose.

At Courtney's funeral, they decided to acknowledge the reality that redefined their lives: Their bright, beautiful daughter, just 20, who played the French horn in high school and dreamed of living in Hawaii, had been kicked out of the Marines for drugs. Eventually, she overdosed at her boyfriend's grandmother's house, where she died alone.

"When I was a kid, junkies were the worst," Doug Griffin, 63, Courtney's father, recalled in their comfortable home here in southeastern New Hampshire. "I used to have an office in New York City. I saw them."

Noting that "junkies" is a word he would never use now, he said that these days, "they're working right next to you and you don't even know it. They're in my daughter's bedroom — they are my daughter."

When the nation's long-running war against drugs was defined by the crack epidemic and based in poor, predominantly black urban areas, the public response was defined by zero tolerance and stiff prison sentences. But today's heroin crisis is different. While heroin use has climbed among all demographic groups, it has skyrocketed among whites; nearly 90 percent of those who tried heroin for the first time in the last decade were white.

And the growing army of families of those lost to heroin — many of them in the suburbs and small towns — are now using their influence, anger and grief to cushion the country's approach to drugs, from altering the language around addiction to prodding government to treat it not as a crime, but as a disease.

Amanda Jordan with her son Brett Honor outside a meeting for people with addictions and their families in Plaistow, N.H. Her son Christopher died of an overdose.

"Because the demographic of people affected are more white, more middle class, these are parents who are empowered," said Michael Botticelli, director of the White House Office of National Drug Control Policy, better known as the nation's drug czar. "They know how to call a legislator, they know how to get angry with their insurance company, they know how to advocate. They have been so instrumental in changing the conversation."

Mr. Botticelli, a recovering alcoholic who has been sober for 26 years, speaks to some of these parents regularly.

Their efforts also include lobbying statehouses, holding rallies and starting nonprofit organizations, making these mothers and fathers part of a growing backlash against the harsh tactics of traditional drug enforcement. These days, in rare bipartisan or even nonpartisan agreement, punishment is out and compassion is in.

The presidential candidates of both parties are now talking about the drug epidemic, with Hillary Rodham Clinton hosting forums on the issue as Jeb Bush and Carly Fiorina tell their own stories of loss while calling for more care and empathy.

Last week, President Obama traveled to West Virginia, a mostly white state with high levels of overdoses, to discuss his $133 million proposal to expand access for drug treatment and prevention programs. The Justice Department is also preparing to release roughly 6,000 inmates from federal prisons as part of an effort to roll back the severe penalties issued to nonviolent drug dealers in decades past.

And in one of the most striking shifts in this new era, some local police departments have stopped punishing many heroin users. In Gloucester, Mass., those who walk into the police station and ask for help, even if they are carrying drugs or needles, are no longer arrested. Instead, they are diverted to treatment, despite questions about the police departments' unilateral authority to do so. It is an approach being replicated by three dozen other police departments around the country.

"How these policies evolve in the first place, and the connection with race, seems very stark," said Marc Mauer, executive director of the Sentencing Project, which examines racial issues in the criminal justice system.

Still, he and other experts said, a broad consensus seems to be emerging: The drug problem will not be solved by arrests alone, but rather by treatment.

Parents like the Griffins say that while they recognize the racial shift in heroin use, politicians and law enforcement are responding in this new way because "they realized what they were doing wasn't working."

"They're paying more attention because people are screaming about it," Mr. Griffin said. "I work with 100 people every day — parents, people in recovery, addicts — who are invading the statehouse, doing everything we can to make as much noise as we can to try to save these kids."

AN EPIDEMIC'S NEW TERRAIN

Heroin's spread into the suburbs and small towns grew out of an earlier wave of addiction to prescription painkillers; together the two trends are ravaging the country.

Deaths from heroin rose to 8,260 in 2013, quadrupling since 2000 and aggravating what some were already calling the worst drug overdose epidemic in United States history.

Over all, drug overdoses now cause more deaths than car crashes, with opioids like OxyContin and other pain medications killing 44 people a day.

Here in New England, the epidemic has grabbed officials by the lapels.

The old industrial cities, quiet small towns and rural outposts are seeing a near-daily parade of drug summit meetings, task forces, vigils against heroin, pronouncements from lawmakers and news media reports on the heroin crisis.

New Hampshire is typical of the hardest-hit states. Last year, 325 people here died of opioid overdoses, a 68 percent increase from 2013. Potentially hundreds more deaths were averted by emergency medical workers, who last year administered naloxone, a medication that reverses the effects of opioid overdoses, in more than 1,900 cases.

Adding to the anxiety among parents, the state also ranks second to last, ahead only of Texas, in access to treatment programs; New Hampshire has about 100,000 people in need of treatment, state officials say, but the state's publicly financed system can serve just 4 percent of them.

Since New Hampshire holds the first-in-the-nation presidential primary, residents have repeatedly raised the issue of heroin with the 2016 candidates.

Mrs. Clinton still recalls her surprise that the first question she was asked in April, at her first open meeting in New Hampshire as a candidate, was not about the economy or health care, but heroin. Last month, she laid out a $10 billion plan to combat and treat drug addiction over the next decade.

Courtney Griffin's father, Doug Griffin, in her bedroom, which he kept unchanged after her death. "We've pretty much given up what used to be our life," he said.

She has also led discussions on the topic around the country, including packed forums like the one in Laconia, N.H., where hundreds of politically engaged, mostly white middle-class men and women, stayed for two hours in a sweltering meeting hall to talk and listen. One woman told of the difficulties of getting her son into a good treatment program, and said he eventually took his own life. Another told Mrs. Clinton of the searing pain of losing her beloved son to heroin.

Many of the 15 Republican candidates for president have heard similar stories, and they are sharing their own.

"I have some personal experience with this as a dad, and it is the most heartbreaking thing in the world to have to go through," Jeb Bush, the former governor of Florida, said at a town hall-style meeting in Merrimack, N.H., in August. His daughter, Noelle, was jailed twice while in rehab, for being caught with prescription pills and accused of having crack cocaine.

Carly Fiorina, the former chief executive of Hewlett-Packard, tells audiences that she and her husband "buried a child to addiction." And Gov. Chris Christie of New Jersey released an ad here in New Hampshire declaring, "We need to be pro-life for the 16-year-old drug addict who's laying on the floor of the county jail."

Some black scholars said they welcomed the shift, while expressing frustration that earlier calls by African-Americans for a more empathetic approach were largely ignored.

"This new turn to a more compassionate view of those addicted to heroin is welcome," said Kimberlé Williams Crenshaw, who specializes in racial issues at Columbia and U.C.L.A. law schools. "But," she added, "one cannot help notice that had this compassion existed for African-Americans caught up in addiction and the behaviors it produces, the devastating impact of mass incarceration upon entire communities would never have happened."

Now, all the political engagement around heroin has helped create what Timothy Rourke, the chairman of the New Hampshire Governor's Commission on Alcohol and Drug Abuse, says is an impetus for change, not unlike the confluence of events that finally produced a response to the AIDS epidemic. "You have a lot of people dying, it's no longer just 'those people,' " he said. "You have people with lived experience demanding better treatment, and you have really good data."

A MORE FORGIVING APPROACH

Among recent bills passed by the New Hampshire legislature in response is one that gives friends and family access to naloxone, the anti-overdose medication. Mr. Griffin, a few months after his daughter died, was among those testifying for the bill. It was set to pass in May but would not take effect until January 2016 — until Mr. Griffin warned lawmakers that too many lives could be lost in that six-month gap. At his urging, the bill was amended to take effect as soon as it was signed into law. It went into effect June 2.

Other parents like him have successfully lobbied for similar measures across the country. Almost all states now have laws or pilot programs making it easier for emergency medical workers or family and friends to obtain naloxone. And 32 states have passed "good Samaritan" laws that protect people from prosecution, at least for low-level offenses, if they call 911 to report an overdose. A generation ago when civil rights activists denounced as racist the push to punish crack-cocaine crimes, largely involving blacks, far more severely than powder-cocaine crimes, involving whites, political figures of both parties defended those policies as necessary to control violent crime.

But today, with heroin ravaging largely white communities in the Northeast and Midwest, and with violent crime largely down, the mood is more forgiving.

"Both the image and reality is that this is a white and often middle-class problem," said Mr. Mauer of the Sentencing Project. "And appropriately so, we're having a much broader conversation about prevention and treatment, and trying to be constructive in responding to this problem. This is good. I don't think we should lock up white kids to show we're being equal."

So officers like Eric Adams, a white former undercover narcotics detective in Laconia, are finding new ways to respond. He is deployed full time now by the Police Department to reach out to people who have overdosed and help them get treatment.

"The way I look at addiction now is completely different," Mr. Adams said. "I can't tell you what changed inside of me, but these are people and they have a purpose in life and we can't as law enforcement look at them any other way. They are committing crimes to feed their addiction, plain and simple. They need help."

Often working with the police, rather than against them, parents are driving these kinds of individual conversions.

Their efforts include attempts to recast addiction in a less stigmatizing light — many parents along with treatment providers are avoiding words like "addict" or "junkie" and instead using terms that convey a chronic illness, like "substance use disorder."

Parents are involved in many ways. To further raise awareness, Jim Hood, 63, of Westport, Conn., who lost his son, Austin, 20, to heroin three years ago, and Greg Williams, 31, of Danbury, Conn., who is in long-term recovery from substance abuse, organized the Oct. 4 "Unite to Face Addiction" rally in Washington. Featuring musicians like Sheryl Crow, it brought together more than 750 groups that are now collaborating to create a national organization, Facing Addiction, devoted to fighting the disease of addiction on the scale of the American Cancer Society and the American Heart Association.

"With heart disease or cancer, you know what to do, who to call, where to go," Mr. Hood said. "With addiction, you just feel like you're out in the Wild West."

Ginger Katz of Norwalk, Conn., has equally lofty goals. After her son, Ian, 20, died of a heroin overdose in 1996, she founded the Courage to Speak Foundation to try to end the silence surrounding addiction, and she has developed a drug-prevention curriculum for schools.

For Doug and Pam Griffin Courtney is still their focus; her pastel bedroom is as she left it, with the schedules of meetings of Narcotics Anonymous taped to what she called her "recovery wall."

"We've pretty much given up what used to be our life," Mr. Griffin said.

But in addition to grieving and testifying at hearings and forums, the Griffins take calls day and night from parents across the country who have read their story and want to offer an encouraging word or ask for advice. They are establishing a sober house, named after Courtney. And they host a potluck dinner and church service once a month on Sunday nights at the First Baptist Church in nearby Plaistow, where they held their daughter's funeral, for people with addictions and their families.

At last month's service, more than 75 people filled the pews, including the family of Christopher Honor, who was Courtney's boyfriend.

He was also addicted to heroin. Last month, almost a year after her death, Chris, 22, died of an overdose — the 23rd overdose and third fatal one this year in Plaistow, a town of 8,000 people.

Chris's mother, Amanda Jordan, 40, wanted to attend the Sunday night service last month, but it was just two weeks after she had buried Chris, and she worried it might be too soon to go back to that church, where Chris's funeral was held. She sometimes thinks Chris is still alive, and at his funeral she was convinced he was still breathing.

She was afraid she would fall apart, but she and other family members decided to go anyway. During the service, her son Brett, 18, became so overwhelmed with emotion that he had to leave, rushing down the center aisle for the outside. Ms. Jordan ran after him. Then a family friend, Shane Manning, ran after both of them. Outside, they all clutched one another and sobbed.

"I'm a mess," Ms. Jordan said after coming back inside and kneeling in front of a picture of Chris. In addition to yearning for her son, she had been worried that the Griffins blamed her for Courtney's death. But at the church, they welcomed her. In their shared pain, the families spoke and embraced.

Ms. Jordan, one of the more recent involuntary members of this club of shattered parents, said that someday, when she is better able to function, she "absolutely" wants to work with the Griffins to "help New Hampshire realize there's a huge problem." Right now, though, she just wants to hunt down the person who sold Chris his fatal dose. "These dealers aren't just selling it," she said. "They're murdering people."

Addiction Treatment Grew Under Health Law. Now What?

BY KATHARINE Q. SEELYE AND ABBY GOODNOUGH | FEB. 10, 2017

MANCHESTER, N.H. — Chad Diaz began using heroin when he was 12. Now 36 and newly covered by Medicaid under the Affordable Care Act, he is on Suboxone, a substitute opioid that eases withdrawal symptoms and cravings, and he is slowly pulling himself together.

"This is the best my life has gone in many, many years," Mr. Diaz, a big man wearing camouflage, said as he sat in a community health center here.

If Congress and President Trump succeed in dismantling the Affordable Care Act, he will have no insurance to pay for his medication or counseling, and he fears he will slide back to heroin.

"If this gets taken from me, it's right back to Square 1," he said. "And that's not a good place. I'm scary when I'm using. I don't care who I hurt."

As the debate over the fate of the health law intensifies, proponents have focused on the lifesaving care it has brought to people with cancer, diabetes and other physical illnesses. But the law has also had a profound, though perhaps less heralded, effect on mental health and addiction treatment, vastly expanding access to those services by designating them as "essential benefits" that must be covered through the A.C.A. marketplaces and expanded Medicaid.

The Center on Budget and Policy Priorities, a left-leaning research group, calculates that 2.8 million people with substance use disorders, including 220,000 with opioid disorders, have coverage under the A.C.A. As the opioid epidemic continues to devastate communities nationwide, public health officials say the law has begun to make a critical difference in their ability to treat and rehabilitate people.

"Of all the illnesses, this is one where we've seen very dramatic changes and where we stand to lose the most ground if we lose the A.C.A.," said Linda Rosenberg, president and chief executive of the National Council for Behavioral Health, adding that treatment programs have begun to be integrated into primary care clinics and health care systems nationwide.

During the presidential campaign, Mr. Trump pledged to rid the country of Obamacare but also to address the opioid epidemic and expand access to drug treatment. Many of the states hardest hit by opioids — including Ohio, West Virginia and Kentucky — voted for Mr. Trump, but some Republican governors have expressed concern about what might happen to people being treated for addiction if their party repeals or scales back the health law.

John Kasich, the Republican governor of Ohio, where the Medicaid expansion has covered 700,000 people, has been particularly outspoken about its success in his state. "Thank God we expanded Medicaid because that Medicaid money is helping to rehab people," Mr. Kasich said during a bill signing in January.

There is still a long way to go. Waiting lists for treatment persist, and many people still lack access, particularly in the 19 states that have opted not to expand Medicaid. Nationwide, 78 people die every day from opioid overdoses, according to the surgeon general, and the number is still rising. And paradoxically, even as the number of opioid prescriptions in the United States has finally started falling, expanded health coverage has probably made it easier for some people to obtain the drugs.

"There's no doubt in my mind that improving access to health care during an era in which opioids are being overprescribed would lead to more addiction," said Dr. Andrew Kolodny, the director of Physicians for Responsible Opioid Prescribing and an addiction specialist.

While 23 million Americans suffer from a substance use disorder, the surgeon general said in a report last year that only one in 10 was receiving treatment as of 2014, the first year people got coverage through the health law. "Now what we're doing is playing catch-up," said Michael Botticelli, director of the White House Office of National Drug Control Policy during the last two years of the Obama administration.

In the past, a third of private insurance plans sold on the individual market did not cover addiction treatment, according to federal health officials, and those that did imposed strict limits. Medicaid covered little besides inpatient detox. Now, more health care providers are offering and getting reimbursed for outpatient counseling and medications like Suboxone and Vivitrol, which have been shown to reduce the potential for relapse.

The health law encourages primary care doctors to incorporate addiction treatment into their practices. It provided grants to several hundred community health centers around the country, many in rural areas, to begin or expand mental health and medication-assisted treatment, which combines counseling and drugs like Suboxone.

This is a big improvement from the days when treatment typically was offered through scattered, poorly funded stand-alone clinics that did not necessarily provide evidence-based treatment and had long waiting lists, said Richard Frank, a professor of health economics at Harvard Medical School.

"The whole system is being pushed more toward looking like modern health care," said Dr. Frank, who worked at the Department of Health and Human Services in the Obama administration.

The 21st Century Cures Act, which Congress passed in December with strong bipartisan support, could build on the progress by providing $1 billion nationwide over the next two years to expand drug treatment around the country, with an emphasis on medication-assisted treatment. The federal government will soon begin distributing the money to states, which will allot it to treatment programs, particularly in high-need areas. But if people lose their insurance, Dr. Frank said, they may well lose access to these new options.

In Kentucky about 11,000 people were receiving addiction treatment through Medicaid by mid-2016, up sharply from 1,500 people in early 2014, according to the Foundation for a Healthy Kentucky, a health policy research group. In West Virginia, Ms. Rosenberg of the National Council for Behavioral Health said, her group's member organizations — nonprofit providers of mental health and addiction treatment — are now treating 30,000 people a year, up from 9,000 before the health law.

Here in New Hampshire — which Mr. Trump won resoundingly in the Republican primary and lost by a hair in November — more than 10,000 people have received addiction treatment after gaining coverage through the Medicaid expansion, said Michele Merritt, senior vice president and policy director at New Futures, a nonprofit advocacy group. Small treatment centers throughout the state that had never been able to bill insurance before have started doing so, she said, allowing them to hire more counselors and accept more patients.

"We're just beginning to implement these exchanges in a way that people know about them," said Senator Jeanne Shaheen, a New Hampshire Democrat, referring to the exchanges created under the health law. Getting rid of them, she said, "makes no sense."

Others note that even with more treatment options, the number of deaths in places like New Hampshire continues to rise. The state ranks first nationwide in per capita overdose deaths from fentanyl, a powerful synthetic opioid that is now killing more people here than heroin. Republicans here have also criticized state health officials for not tracking how many Medicaid enrollees who receive addiction treatment end up relapsing.

In Pennsylvania, where 124,000 people have received addiction treatment under the Medicaid expansion, health officials were disturbed by early data showing that two-thirds of those who went to detox got no other treatment services. So Gov. Tom Wolf, a Democrat, is designating 45 "Centers of Excellence" — primary care clinics where people can also get addiction and mental health treatment, with frequent follow-up and a team of providers closely tracking their progress.

The new model is in use here at the Manchester Community Health Center, where Mr. Diaz receives treatment. The center had offered minimal services for substance abuse before the health law.

Now, three years later, it has undergone substantial changes. More than 40 percent of its patients had been uninsured; today, only 20 percent are. The center used to have one building, a staff of 55 and 7,500 patients; today, it has clinics in four locations, a staff of 230 and more than 16,000 patients, about 800 of whom have substance abuse issues.

It has two providers who are licensed to prescribe medication-assisted treatment, which it is expanding to 60 patients, including pregnant women, the center's priority. "The number may sound low as far as how many we're treating," said Julie Hazell-Felch, director of behavioral health at the center. "But it's a multitude of services they're receiving and they're in here weekly," she said, seeing nurses, a behavioral health clinician and a medical provider, and giving urine samples and receiving their medications.

If the Affordable Care Act is repealed, the center stands to lose more than $6 million in funding, mostly Medicaid revenue, about a third of its $18 million annual budget.

"We would not be able to keep all four sites open," said Kris McCracken, president and chief executive of the health center.

She added: "There are only two avenues to go: You either prevent and treat, or you street. That's what will happen. People will end up back on the street."

KATHARINE Q. SEELYE REPORTED FROM MANCHESTER, N.H., AND ABBY GOODNOUGH FROM WASHINGTON.

Attorney General Orders Tougher Sentences, Rolling Back Obama Policy

BY REBECCA R. RUIZ | MAY 12, 2017

WASHINGTON — Attorney General Jeff Sessions has ordered federal prosecutors to pursue the toughest possible charges and sentences against crime suspects, he announced Friday, reversing Obama administration efforts to ease penalties for some nonviolent drug violations.

The drastic shift in criminal justice policy, foreshadowed during recent weeks, is Mr. Sessions's first major stamp on the Justice Department, and it highlights several of his top targets: drug dealing, gun crime and gang violence.

In an eight-paragraph memo, Mr. Sessions returned to the guidance of President George W. Bush's administration by calling for more uniform punishments — including mandatory minimum sentences — and instructing prosecutors to pursue the harshest possible charges. Mr. Sessions's policy is broader than that of the Bush administration, however, and how it is carried out will depend more heavily on the judgments of United States attorneys and assistant attorneys general as they bring charges.

The policy signaled a return to "enforcing the laws that Congress has passed," Mr. Sessions said Friday at the Justice Department, characterizing his memo as unique for the leeway it afforded prosecutors.

"They deserve to be un-handcuffed and not micromanaged from Washington," he said. "It means we are going to meet our responsibility to enforce the law with judgment and fairness."

But Mr. Sessions's memo also highlighted the gulf between his views on sentencing and a growing bipartisan push for an overhaul of the criminal justice system. A major reform bill gained steam in

Congress last year but foundered amid congressional dysfunction and Donald J. Trump's campaign push for what he termed a restoration of law and order. Numerous states have also enacted overhauls to their criminal justice systems in recent years.

Even some within the Republican Party criticized Mr. Sessions. Senator Mike Lee of Utah labeled an overhaul of the criminal justice system a conservative issue. "To be tough on crime, we have to be smart on crime," he wrote on Twitter.

Freedom Partners, an action fund partly funded by the conservative Koch brothers, advocated changes to the law and pointed to the failed legislation as a place to start anew.

Senator Tom Cotton, an Arkansas Republican who spoke out last year against the overhaul legislation, backed the new directive. "I agree with Attorney General Sessions that law enforcement should side with the victims of crime rather than its perpetrators," he said.

Mr. Sessions's memo replaced the orders of former Attorney General Eric H. Holder Jr., who in 2013 took aim at drug sentencing rules. He encouraged prosecutors to consider the individual circumstances of a case and to exercise discretion in charging drug crimes. In cases of nonviolent defendants with insignificant criminal histories and no connections to criminal organizations, Mr. Holder instructed prosecutors to omit details about drug quantities from charging documents so as not to trigger automatically harsh penalties.

Mr. Holder called Mr. Sessions's policy "unwise and ill-informed," saying in a statement that it ignored the consensus between Democrats and Republicans to overhaul the criminal justice system and also rejected data demonstrating that prosecutions of high-level drug defendants had risen under his guidance.

"This absurd reversal is driven by voices who have not only been discredited but until now have been relegated to the fringes of this debate," he said.

Mr. Sessions's memo explicitly mentioned Mr. Holder's 2013 directive in a footnote and rescinded it effective immediately.

The policy is most similar to one issued by Attorney General John Ashcroft in 2003. Then, Mr. Ashcroft outlined six types of "limited exceptions" in his memo — which ran nearly four times the length of Mr. Sessions's new guidance, and repeatedly referred to certain federal statutes. Mr. Sessions, by contrast, provided few specifics.

Instead, he simply directed prosecutors to "carefully consider whether an exception may be justified." He said any such exceptions to ease criminal penalties must be documented and approved by United States attorneys, assistant attorneys general or their designees.

Kevin H. Sharp, who until last month was a federal judge for the Middle District of Tennessee, warned that a lack of specifics could hold back prosecutors from exercising discretion when it might be warranted.

"You don't know what the exception is, so it makes it harder to justify it," he said. "You have to write a memo and run it up for approval — you're going to get fewer people doing that."

Mr. Sessions has said he believes that critics of mandatory minimum sentences are ignoring the Justice Department's duty to enforce federal law.

David Alan Sklansky, a law professor at Stanford University who specializes in criminal justice, disagreed in part. "Not everybody who falls within the letter of the criminal prohibition is somebody who deserves that kind of criminal punishment," he said. "It's not about excusing people or condoning criminal behavior; it's a question of trying to figure out how much punishment is enough and at what point are you piling on needlessly and at great cost."

Mr. Sessions has argued that violent crimes such as murder can be an outgrowth of drug crime, and has suggested that prosecuting drug crimes more vigorously will reduce crime more broadly.

"Many violent crimes are driven by drug trafficking and drug-trafficking organizations," Mr. Sessions, who was a prosecutor at the height of the 1980s crack epidemic, wrote in a March 8 memo.

Mr. Sklansky said it was unclear how dramatic an impact Mr. Sessions's new policy may have.

"Prosecutors in the field appropriately pay attention to and try to follow the directions they receive from Washington," he said. "A reversal or replacement of the Holder memo will be interpreted by many prosecutors in the field as a direction to be more aggressive to use mandatory minimum penalties against low-level nonviolent drug offenders.

"It's hard to know how much of an effect it will have," he added, "but it will have an effect."

When Opioid Addicts Find an Ally in Blue

BY AL BAKER | **JUNE 12, 2017**

Across the country, police leaders are assigning themselves a big role in reversing a complex crisis, and not through mass arrests.

BURLINGTON, VT. — In this college town on the banks of Lake Champlain, Chief Brandon del Pozo has hired a plain-spoken social worker to oversee opioids policy and has begun mapping heroin deaths the way his former commanders in the New York Police Department track crime.

In New York City, detectives are investigating overdoses with the rigor of homicides even if murder charges are a long shot. They are plying the mobile phones of the dead for clues about suppliers and using telltale marks on heroin packages and pills to trace them back to dealers. And like their colleagues in Philadelphia and Ohio, they are racing to issue warnings about deadly strains of drugs when bodies fall, the way epidemiologists take on Zika.

The police in Arlington, Mass., intervene with vulnerable users. Officials in Everett, Wash., have sued a pharmaceutical firm that they say created a black market for addicts. Seattle's officers give low-level drug and prostitution suspects a choice: treatment instead of arrest and jail.

Opioids are cutting through the country, claiming increasing deaths and, in some cities, wrecking more lives than traffic fatalities and murders combined. Police leaders are weary of the scenes: 911 calls; bodies with needles in their arms; drugs called "fire" strewn about. They are assigning themselves a big role in reversing the problems. They are working with public health officials, and carrying more antidote for heroin and its synthetic cousin fentanyl.

Few see policing, by itself, as the answer to such a complex social problem, certainly not through enforcement alone. The law enforcement

Chief Brandon del Pozo of the Burlington police said his city had dealt with a constant flow of illegal drugs.

approach to the crack-cocaine scourge of the late 1980s filled jails and prisons, expanded government and did little to address the social issues driving that addiction crisis.

"The police can play a critical role in a very broadly based social and medical response," said Samuel Walker, an emeritus professor of criminal justice at the University of Nebraska Omaha. "So if people think we are going to arrest our way out of the opioid crisis, they're wrong."

Governors like Andrew M. Cuomo of New York and Chris Christie of New Jersey, both former prosecutors, have adopted a notably compassionate tone in framing the crisis. In 2014, Gov. Peter Shumlin of Vermont used 34 minutes of his state-of-the state speech to urge treatment and support for addicts. As a candidate, President Trump vowed to solve America's drug crisis, a pledge that resonated in impoverished, rural areas that have been ravaged in recent years by opioids.

Labeling it a health epidemic, not a war on drugs, marks a stark contrast with the criminal justice system's approach to the crack-cocaine plague, which was met by mass arrests in mostly black and Hispanic communities.

Now, policing leaders claim to have learned from the past. But they also know how violent crime can flow from illegal drugs the way Anthony Riccio, a chief in the Chicago Police Department, says is happening in his city. A big fear among police chiefs is that increased demand for low-cost, high-potency opioids will lead to more shootings, and murders, as prices drop and drug traffickers organize.

In Mexico, where almost all of the heroin entering the United States is grown and cultivated, violence surrounding the drug trade is "horrific," said Chuck Rosenberg, who runs the Drug Enforcement Administration.

But American cities are not immune.

"In almost all of our major seizures and arrests, we're encountering weapons," Mr. Rosenberg said. "And there's only one reason to have those around."

Increasingly, the police find themselves scrambling from call to call for reports of seemingly lifeless bodies. Death counts are rising. Nearly 1,400 people died of drug overdoses in New York City last year, the highest ever and up from 937 the previous year. In Philadelphia, the tally was 906. Nationally, there were 52,000 overdose deaths in 2015, Mr. Rosenberg said. And last year, the drug overdose death count likely exceeded 59,000, according to preliminary data compiled by The New York Times.

Despite the daily toll, no single loss has seemed to galvanize collective concern or outrage, and some fear that a kind of compassion fatigue is setting in.

"Where is the Len Bias moment?" asked Chuck Wexler, the executive director of the Police Executive Research Forum, referring to the college basketball star's cocaine-overdose death in 1986, considered a starting point for a so-called national war on drugs.

Burlington law enforcement officers arresting a man who swallowed a bag of heroin and tried to swallow a second, seen on the trunk of the car.

"We've been at this for, now, four or five years, and the overdose numbers continue to go up," he added. "What's going to be the defining moment to move this in a different direction?"

To that end, Mr. Wexler brought scores of local law enforcement leaders together last month to confront a battle that J.Scott Thomson, the police chief in Camden, N.J., told them "we are still losing." In an auditorium at 1 Police Plaza in Lower Manhattan, attendees spoke with prosecutors and public health officials of the new tactics and realignments the crisis has wrought.

They discussed the "good Samaritan" laws that grant overdose victims seeking medical help immunity from prosecution, and how sheriffs can get help for addicted inmates. But each idea seemed a friction point: How to tell a midlevel dealer from a user needing help? How to tie a specific drug to a death to bring a murder charge? How to choke off supply routes that begin beyond their borders? How to use more discretion on nonviolent drug violators when Attorney General Jeff Sessions is ordering the harshest possible charges in federal drug cases.

It is a complex crisis, with roots in years of overprescription and abuse of opioid pills, which hooked people around the nation, Mr. Rosenberg said. "Roughly four out of five new heroin users start out on prescription medication," he said.

On the street, heroin can be one-fifth the price of opioid pills like hydrocodone and oxycodone. It is also a more plentiful substitute, Mr. Rosenberg said, and can be far more potent, particularly with the emergence of strains mixed with fentanyl and carfentanyl.

In New York City, Robert K. Boyce, the chief of detectives, saw overdose deaths hitting record highs in areas across the city. This as homicides dropped to 335 last year and traffic fatalities to 220. He created new teams of homicide and narcotics detectives to focus on how sales — usually of $10 bags or $100 bundles — occur via digital links, and "not on the street," and added 84 investigators to the effort.

On the streets, 17,000 of the city's 23,000 patrol officers have been trained in the use of naloxone, a drug that reverses opioid overdoses. And when people do die, patrol officers "freeze the scene like it's a homicide case," he said.

"Everything is data-driven," the chief said. "Their last phone number is usually their provider. So now you see what else pops off that number. Now you have a nexus."

There is no expectation of privacy for a dead person, so a warrant is not necessary, though the police often seek cooperation from relatives in seeking passwords. The investigators move quickly, even before a cause of death is officially determined. Details from one case can tie it to others.

In Vermont, a constant flow of illegal drugs arrives in cars driven from New York, Chief del Pozo and his investigators said. Couriers hide drugs in body cavities and alter their routes, coming up Interstate 91 or the New York State Thruway, veering east at Fort Ann, N.Y., and into Vermont's southern region.

Chief del Pozo, left, and Officer Campbell spoke with a Shopping Bag customer.

Burlington, 50 miles from Canada, is often their last stop. There, the drug couriers find hosts who help distribute drugs: pills, bulk heroin and, increasingly, fentanyl.

On a recent day, Lt. Michael Warren steered a police car along the tree-lined streets of the city's Old North End, tracing a path of wreckage.

Here, on Ward Street, two brothers overdosed last June in chairs on their front porch. There, on Hyde Street, a genetics major at the University of Vermont was discovered dead. A sign for a corner store, at North and Rose Streets, marks the spot of a drive-by shooting over drugs two summers ago. A block away, at North and LaFountain Streets, an open-air drug bazaar once reigned.

"It's all around," Lieutenant Warren said as a man who he said had overdosed several times bicycled by.

But the area has changed since the police started regular foot patrols, put 140-watt LED bulbs in the streetlights and encouraged merchants to do the same. Now drugs are not as visible, said Doug

Olsaver, who has worked for 20 years as a manager at the Shopping Bag, a store at LaFountain and North Streets.

"An officer told me that his opinion of drug dealers were that they were like cockroaches," Mr. Olsaver said. "They hate light."

Earlier that day, Chief del Pozo took a seat with Jackie Corbally — whose title with the Burlington Police Department is opiate policy coordinator, but he calls her the drug czar — at a U-shaped set of tables at the Police Headquarters in the neighboring town of Winooski. The meeting, called SubStat, began convening regularly four months ago with the goal of tracking dozens of vulnerable users who have either been arrested or overdosed. It is based on New York's computerized crime fighting system, CompStat, but broader, with those in corrections and parole, the prosecutor's office and public health in on the talks with local police leaders.

"It's all about shifting from addiction as a crime to addiction as a disease," said Jane Helmstetter of the state's human services agency, who was at the meeting.

One Burlington man, with a longtime addiction and a record of arrests, was struggling to believe the police could help him, he said, even after an officer revived him in April, after his second of three overdoses in 10 days. The officer followed him to a hospital emergency room and told him, "If you need help, we'll drive you to treatment right now."

Soon, the man met Ms. Corbally, and found himself face to face with Chief del Pozo, an unlikely ally. They helped get him into rehabilitation. The encounter was surprising, said the man and his mother, who have tried to keep their ordeal private and spoke on the condition that their names not be published.

"He wasn't just treated as a drug addict and someone that wasn't worthy of help," his mother said. "Here you have a police chief sitting in the same room with a drug addict that knowingly uses illegal substances and he's not going to handcuff him? It was unusual."

White House Panel Recommends Declaring National Emergency on Opioids

BY ABBY GOODNOUGH | JULY 31, 2017

WASHINGTON — President Trump's commission on the opioid crisis asked him Monday to declare a national emergency to deal with the epidemic.

The members of the bipartisan panel called the request their "first and most urgent recommendation."

Mr. Trump created the commission in March, appointing Gov. Chris Christie of New Jersey to lead it. The panel held its first public meeting last month and was supposed to issue an interim report shortly afterward but delayed doing so until now. A final report is due in October.

"With approximately 142 Americans dying every day, America is enduring a death toll equal to Sept. 11 every three weeks," the commission members wrote, referring to the 9/11 terrorist attacks. "Your declaration would empower your cabinet to take bold steps and would force Congress to focus on funding and empowering the executive branch even further to deal with this loss of life."

In addition to seeking an emergency declaration, the commission proposed waiving a federal rule that sharply limits the number of Medicaid recipients who can receive residential addiction treatment.

It also called for expanding access to medications that help treat opioid addiction, requiring "prescriber education initiatives" and providing model legislation for states to allow a standing order for anyone to receive naloxone, a drug used to reverse opioid overdoses.

Some public health experts said the main effect of declaring an emergency would be to make Americans regard the epidemic more urgently.

"It's really about drawing attention to the issue and pushing for all hands on deck," said Michael Fraser, the executive director of the Association of State and Territorial Health Officials. "It would allow a level of attention and coordination that the federal agencies might not otherwise have, but in terms of day-to-day lifesaving, I don't think it would make much difference."

The governors of Arizona, Florida, Maryland and Virginia have declared states of emergency regarding the opioid addiction crisis; in Alaska, Gov. Bill Walker has issued a disaster declaration.

In addition to Mr. Christie, the members of the commission are Gov. Charlie Baker of Massachusetts (a Republican), Gov. Roy Cooper of North Carolina (a Democrat), Patrick Kennedy, a former congressman from Rhode Island (a Democrat), and Bertha K. Madras, a Harvard Medical School professor who specializes in addiction biology.

Dr. Tom Frieden, the director of the Centers for Disease Control and Prevention during the Obama administration, said declaring a public health emergency under the Stafford Act, as the commission recommended, was usually reserved for natural disasters like hurricanes.

"This is not a natural disaster; it's one caused by overprescription of opiates and flooding of illegal opiates into the country," Dr. Frieden said. "The critical measures for reversing the opioid epidemic are improving prescribing and increasing interdiction of illicit opioids."

Gary Mendell, the founder and chief executive of Shatterproof, an anti-addiction advocacy group, said an emergency declaration would be "a significant first step towards acknowledging the severity of the crisis we face and the urgent need for action, including national emergency funding and suspending regulatory hurdles that limit our ability to save lives."

Mr. Cooper said in a statement that he considered the report "incomplete when it comes to making sure all Americans have access to affordable health care, which includes mental health and substance abuse treatment." He added, "I urge the commission to make a stronger stand on the accessibility and affordability of health care."

This Judge Has a Mission: Keep Defendants Alive

BY TIMOTHY WILLIAMS | JAN. 3, 2018

BUFFALO — There are two kinds of defendants who enter Judge Craig D. Hannah's courtroom: Those who stand on the far side of the bench to have their cases considered in the usual way, and those invited to step closer. Close enough to shake the judge's hand or shout obscenities in his face, depending on their mood that day.

Both kinds are facing criminal charges, but those in the second group have volunteered to take part in an experiment where the primary goal is to save their lives. Arrested for crimes related to addiction, they are participants in what is believed to be the nation's first opioid court.

Unlike typical drug courts, which can end in punishment if defendants relapse, this one recognizes that failure is part of the recovery process.

Its measure of success — preventing death — is arguably a low bar. Then again, few initiatives have made much of a dent in an epidemic that is killing more people each year than car accidents do. The criminal justice system may not be the ideal place to address addiction, but the reality is that it is a place where drug users are a captive audience. And the court, by linking with nonprofits, offers treatment for those who could not otherwise afford it. Court systems around the country are watching Buffalo as a potential model.

Participants are required to appear daily before Judge Hannah, who was himself once addicted to drugs. "I'm going to be your new best friend," he tells them. "So I'm going to start calling you by your first name from now on. See you tomorrow. Keep up the good work."

MICHAEL'S STORY

Michael Marcinkowski's right leg twitches nervously. He's high again. When his name is called, he walks nervously toward Judge Hannah

Judge Craig D. Hannah, center, at the Opiate Crisis Intervention Court in Buffalo, N.Y.

until he can no longer avoid looking him in the eye.

"What's going on? This doesn't look too good," the judge says. "This is twice in a week, right?"

Michael, 21, avoids a direct answer. "I've been going to a meeting every day. After the third day, I relapse."

Judge Hannah scans the file and begins speaking, as if to himself. "Did I misread it? Because I went to a public school. I want to make sure I didn't misread it."

The room goes quiet. The young man fidgets. A bailiff is breathing over his shoulder. "See that tall gentleman behind you?" the judge says. "I'm thinking about keeping you."

During a break, Michael says he sets a timer every 15 minutes to interrupt his urge to use. "From midnight to 6 a.m., I'm screaming."

But the judge's options are limited: A locked inpatient treatment center or the Erie County jail. "You may not like that kind of help," he says, telling him to come back tomorrow, clean.

A JUDGE WITH HIS OWN PAST

Judge Hannah is a generation older than most of those who appear in his court. He was once hooked on cocaine, but stopped using drugs in his early 20s.

In court, he does not speak in legal jargon. The defendants are his peers. He talks about the Bills, the city's popular football team, or the cold weather. He asks them how they are feeling, how he can help. He does not hurry anyone along.

Friends ask him why opioid users, who are largely white, get gentler treatment than crack users, who were disproportionately black, did in the 1980s.

"I think we learned," says the judge, who is African-American. "We locked up a generation of young black men, and then when they get out, they are dumped back in a community with no marketable skills. This time, people realized that this ain't just affecting the boys in the 'hood anymore."

His own addiction ruined his chance to become a Marine Corps officer. The night before his military physical to begin officer training, he used cocaine because, he said, "I figured I could never get high again." He didn't count on being drug-tested that morning. He walked out before the results came back.

"There's a shame in addiction. That's one thing we have to remove. Part of recovery is telling people that the only difference between you and them is time."

He presides in a city where the number of opioid overdose deaths, already high in 2015, more than doubled in 2016, to about 300.

But aside from force of personality, he has few tools at his disposal. If defendants continue to use, they are returned to criminal court to face their charges. If they agree to treatment but no beds are available, they have to wait. No one can be required to take medications that would help quell their addictions. But if participants complete the program — which generally means going 60 days without

Defendants wait to speak with Judge Hannah at the court.

drugs — they have a good chance of having their charges reduced or dropped altogether.

Since the project started last May, only one of its 92 participants has died from an overdose. It is too early to tell if the others will stay clean.

Judge Hannah acknowledges that the powerful opioids available now are far more ruthless than the drugs of his youth. "This substance is a monster. It releases all your pleasure receptors all at one time. If the birth of your baby is an 8, and the best sex of your life is a 9.5, the first shot of heroin is a 4,000."

NICHOLAS'S STORY

Nicholas Schuh, 25, says he believed opioid court would be a waste of time. The alternative, though, was a painful detox behind bars. He had not been clean since age 15, when he started by stealing his mother's prescription painkillers. Though he had pledged to avoid shooting up, he eventually cajoled his brother, a heroin user, into injecting him. "I told myself, if I ever shot up, my life would be over."

He wasn't wrong.

He says he lost 10 jobs in a year. He crashed his car. He stole so much that one of his younger brothers finally installed a deadbolt on his own bedroom door. Nicholas overdosed twice; once, he left the hospital to score again.

He was not a fan of Judge Hannah, who thought Nicholas's best hope was to check into a locked inpatient treatment facility, where rules are stricter than in many jails. "I wanted to say, 'Did you go through inpatient?' He's never done that," Nicholas said. "I felt I was being pushed into a corner."

But something finally clicked. He now receives an injection of Vivitrol, a drug that blocks opioid highs, every 30 days and has become a Christian. "He has truly saved my life," he says of Judge Hannah. "We have a relationship. So it isn't like going to see a judge you're scared of." He pauses, surprised by his own words. "I look forward to seeing that man every day."

JUSTIN'S STORY

Last month, when Justin Schmidbauer's best friend died of a heroin overdose, his thoughts turned to getting high, threatening his nearly three months of sobriety.

His life these days is spent seeking distractions from the urge to use: hanging out with his 11-year-old daughter, going fishing, attending 10 Narcotics Anonymous and Alcoholics Anonymous meetings a week.

Justin, 36, refuses to use medications like Suboxone that help curb addiction and save lives. He views a drug-free recovery as a way to win back lost self-worth.

Instead, when he gets a craving for heroin, he mentally plays what he calls "the tape of consequences." If he gets high, the tape goes, " 'Yeah, for five minutes I feel O.K., but everything I've worked for is gone.' "

In court, Judge Hannah says he heard about the death of Justin's friend. "I was thinking about you, but the rules are I can't contact you outside court," the judge says. (To maintain impartiality, judges cannot speak privately with one side of a case, except through a lawyer.)

Weeks later, Judge Hannah announces that Justin has successfully completed the program. Justin's charges, four counts of drug possession, are reduced to a single, noncriminal violation. His fellow defendants give him an ovation. He is on top of the world.

Now comes the hard part.

Justice Dept. Backs High-Stakes Lawsuit Against Opioid Makers

BY KATIE BENNER AND JAN HOFFMAN | FEB. 27, 2018

WASHINGTON — The Justice Department is throwing its weight behind plaintiffs in a sprawling, high-stakes prescription opioids lawsuit in Ohio, Attorney General Jeff Sessions said on Tuesday.

Mr. Sessions said that the Justice Department plans to file a so-called statement of interest in the lawsuit, a technique that past administrations have typically reserved for cases that directly affect the federal government's interests, like diplomacy and national security.

The Obama administration had used statements of interest to expand the boundaries of civil rights laws.

At a news conference, Mr. Sessions said the lawsuit targeted "opioid manufacturers and distributors for allegedly using false, deceptive and unfair marketing of opioid drugs."

He also announced the creation of a task force to pursue the makers and distributors of prescription opioids and said it will "examine existing state and local government lawsuits against opioid manufacturers to determine if we can be of assistance."

"We will use criminal penalties," Mr. Sessions said. "We will use civil penalties. We will use whatever tools we have to hold people accountable for breaking our laws."

The lawsuit pending in Federal District Court in Cleveland consolidates more than 400 complaints by cities, counties and Native American tribes nationwide. They accused manufacturers, distributors and dispensers of prescription opioids of using misleading marketing to promote the painkillers.

The lawsuit also accuses the defendants of playing down the addictiveness of the drugs and failing to report suspicious orders by consumers that would indicate the drugs were being abused.

Some of the high-profile defendants include pharmaceutical giants Johnson & Johnson, Purdue Pharma and Teva Pharmaceuticals, large distributors McKesson and Cardinal Health and pharmacy chains like CVS, Rite Aid and Walgreens.

Mr. Sessions called the opioid addiction crisis "beyond imagining" during separate remarks on Tuesday morning at the National Association of Attorneys General. He said the government would take a hard look at doctors who overprescribe prescription painkillers, which can lead to addiction and abuse of illegal drugs like heroin.

Mr. Sessions has described the opioid epidemic as a national health crisis and estimates that 64,000 Americans died of drug overdoses in 2016, a record increase. The vast majority of those deaths, he said, happened after users took opioids like prescription painkillers, heroin and fentanyl.

He also called the opioid crisis a significant drain on federal resources, costing the government $115 billion in 2017 and $1 trillion since 2001. He predicted that it could cost the United States an additional $500 billion over the next three years.

The attorney general is legally able to argue on behalf of the government's interest in any court in the country via a statement of interest, which does not make the government a plaintiff. Mr. Sessions's announcement on Tuesday followed a significant dispute in the case in Ohio.

On Monday, lawyers for the Drug Enforcement Administration attended a hearing in the Ohio courtroom about how much data they would share about the national distribution of painkillers.

Insisting that it did not want to compromise ongoing criminal investigations, the agency offered to provide two years' worth of information in the case. Judge Dan Aaron Polster has given the agency until next Monday to decide whether it will comply with his request to provide the sides with nine years of data. Determining the number of pills, the location and the distributors can be a major factor in assigning liability.

Richard Fields, a lawyer who represents state attorneys general and sovereign Native American nations in opioid litigation, predicted that the statement of interest "will help unlock this data so that we can hold manufacturers, distributors and pharmacies accountable for flooding communities with pills."

Glossary

Affordable Care Act Healthcare reform law signed by President Barack Obama, which expanded coverage of addiction treatment.

buprenorphine Opioid used as a maintenance therapy for recovering addicts, designed to minimize the euphoria associated with traditional opioids.

carfentanil Animal tranquilizer that is 100 times more potent than fentanyl.

chronic pain Pain symptoms lasting longer than 12 weeks, often treated with opioid painkillers.

drug cartel Criminal organization specializing in the trafficking of illegal drugs.

drug court Court docket designed for drug addicts, providing sentencing alternatives intended to minimize addiction.

Drug Enforcement Agency Federal law enforcement agency tasked with combating illegal drug sales and use.

drug rehabilitation Medical and therapeutic treatment helping recover from addiction to drugs.

fentanyl Rapid onset opioid with high risk of overdose, responsible for spike in fatal drug overdoses during the opioid crisis.

harm reduction Practices that minimize adverse effects of addiction, such as needle exchanges, anti-overdose medication, and safety training.

hydrocodone Opioid painkiller, commonly sold under the brand name Vicodin.

maintenance therapy A medical therapy designed to prevent return to addictive substance, typically involving supervised use of methadone, buprenorphine, or naltrexone.

methadone Opioid used as a maintenance therapy for recovering addicts, commonly administered at specialized clinics.

naloxone Anti-overdose drug, commonly sold under the brand name Narcan, that has become more widespread in the midst of the opioid crisis.

needle exchange Social service offering replacement syringes to intravenous drug users, in order to prevent the transmission of disease by contaminated needles.

opioid Substances based on the opium poppy or with similar effects, commonly used in pain relief and with high risk of addiction.

Opioid and Drug Abuse Commission Commission authorized by President Donald Trump to investigate the causes of the opioid epidemic and make recommendations.

overdose Ingestion of a substance in quantities greater than recommended, risking death or bodily harm.

oxycodone Opioid painkiller, commonly sold under the brand name OxyContin.

post-traumatic stress disorder A state of persistent distress following a traumatic event, often leading to risk of substance abuse.

synthetic opioid Class of opioids mimicking the effects of prescription opioids like morphine and codeine, including fentanyl and carfentanil.

Vivitrol Brand name of naltrexone, medication for treating alcohol or opioid dependence, commonly injected.

withdrawal Symptoms caused by the limitation of drugs, often causing severe physical distress.

Media Literacy Terms

"Media literacy" refers to the ability to access, understand, critically assess, and create media. The following terms are important components of media literacy, and they will help you critically engage with the articles in this title.

angle The aspect of a news story that a journalist focuses on and develops.

attribution The method by which a source is identified or by which facts and information are assigned to the person who provided them.

balance Principle of journalism that both perspectives of an argument should be presented in a fair way.

bias A disposition of prejudice in favor of a certain idea, person, or perspective.

byline Name of the writer, usually placed between the headline and the story.

chronological order Method of writing a story presenting the details of the story in the order in which they occurred.

credibility The quality of being trustworthy and believable, said of a journalistic source.

editorial Article of opinion or interpretation.

feature story Article designed to entertain as well as to inform.

headline Type, usually 18 point or larger, used to introduce a story.

human interest story Type of story that focuses on individuals and how events or issues affect their life, generally offering a sense of relatability to the reader.

impartiality Principle of journalism that a story should not reflect a journalist's bias and should contain balance.

intention The motive or reason behind something, such as the publication of a news story.

interview story Type of story in which the facts are gathered primarily by interviewing another person or persons.

inverted pyramid Method of writing a story using facts in order of importance, beginning with a lead and then gradually adding paragraphs in order of relevance from most interesting to least interesting.

motive The reason behind something, such as the publication of a news story or a source's perspective on an issue.

news story An article or style of expository writing that reports news, generally in a straightforward fashion and without editorial comment.

op-ed An opinion piece that reflects a prominent journalist's opinion on topic of interest.

paraphrase The summary of an individual's words, with attribution, rather than a direct quotation of their exact words.

quotation The use of an individual's exact words indicated by the use of quotation marks and proper attribution.

reliability The quality of being dependable and accurate, said of a journalistic source.

rhetorical device Technique in writing intending to persuade the reader or communicate a message from a certain perspective.

tone A manner of expression in writing or speech.

Media Literacy Questions

1. Compare the headlines of "Drug Deaths in America are Rising Faster than Ever" (on page 30) and " 'The Pills Are Everywhere': How the Opioid Crisis Claims its Youngest Victims" (on page 35). What tone does each establish? How do they set up different kinds of news stories?

2. "The Bronx's Quiet, Brutal War With Opioids" (on page 39) is an example of a human interest story. What perspectives does the article explore, and how does it make them appeal to the reader?

3. "A Foster Child of the Opioid Epidemic" (on page 46), an op-ed by Lisa Marie Basile, is a personal narrative. What is the intention of the piece? What are the goals of the author?

4. "At Clinics, Tumultuous Lives and Turbulent Care" (on page 88) uses direct quotes and paraphrases from multiple interview sources. How is information conveyed differently in these two forms of attribution? What benefit does each form offer that the other does not?

5. "Study Finds Competing Opioid Treatments Have Similar Outcomes" (on page 129) describes conflicting perspectives on the merits of different addiction maintenance drugs. How do the journalists maintain balance in their coverage?

6. In "Tightening the Lid On Pain Prescriptions" (on page 143), Barry Meier draws on various sources. Can you identify them?

7. "How Doctors Helped Drive the Addiction Crisis" (on page 153) is

an op-ed. What makes Richard Friedman's perspective relevant to the issue?

8. "Doctors Will Play a Critical Role in the Opioid Epidemic" (on page 157) is an editorial. What opinion does it advocate, and how does it differ from a news story?

9. "Opioid Addiction Knows No Color, but Its Treatment Does" (on page 134) and "In Heroin Crisis, White Families Seek Gentler War On Drugs" (on page 175) have distinctive tones. Compare and contrast them.

10. In "Attorney General Orders Tougher Sentences, Rolling Back Obama Policy" (on page 189), Rebecca R. Ruiz writes in the "inverted pyramid" style, with the most important information first. Compare the first paragraph with the last. What makes the information in the first paragraph more important?

11. "When Opioid Addicts Find an Ally in Blue" (on page 193) has an angle that focuses the reporting. What is that angle? Can you determine it from the headline?

12. In "This Judge Has a Mission: Keep Defendants Alive" (on page 202), the story is broken into several sections. What information is included in each section? Why is it organized that way?

Citations

All citations in this list are formatted according to the Modern Language Association's (MLA) style guide.

BOOK CITATION

NEW YORK TIMES EDITORIAL STAFF, THE. *The Opioid Epidemic: Tracking A Crisis.* New York Times Educational Publishing, 2019.

ARTICLE CITATIONS

ALVAREZ, LIZETTE. "Haven for Recovering Addicts Now Profits from their Relapses." *The New York Times*, 20 June 2016, https://www.nytimes.com/2017/06/20/us/delray-beach-addiction.html.

BAKER, AL. "When Opioid Addicts Find an Ally in Blue." *The New York Times*, 12 June 2017, https://www.nytimes.com/2017/06/12/nyregion/when-opioid-addicts-find-an-ally-in-blue.html.

BASILE, LISA MARIE. "A Foster Child of the Opioid Epidemic." *The New York Times*, 24 Nov. 2017, https://www.nytimes.com/2017/11/24/well/family/a-foster-child-of-the-opioid-epidemic.html.

BENNER, KATIE AND JAN HOFFMAN. "Justice Department Backs High-Stakes Lawsuit Against Opioid Makers." *The New York Times*, 27 Feb. 2018, https://www.nytimes.com/2018/02/27/us/politics/justice-department-opioid-lawsuit.html.

CAREY, BENEDICT. "Prescription Painkillers Seen As Gateway to Heroin." *The New York Times*, 10 Feb. 2014, https://www.nytimes.com/2014/02/11/health/prescription-painkillers-seen-as-a-gateway-to-heroin.html.

DAO, JAMES. "Some Veterans on Painkillers at Special Risk, A Study Finds." *The New York Times*, 08 March 2012, https://atwar.blogs.nytimes.com/2012/03/07/for-veterans-with-post-traumatic-stress-pain-killers-carry-risks.

DEL REAL, JOSE A. "Opioid Addiction Knows No Color, but Its Treatment Does." *The New York Times*, 12 Jan. 2018, https://www.nytimes.com/2018/01/12/

nyregion/opioid-addiction-knows-no-color-but-its-treatment-does.html.

DEL REAL, JOSE A. "The Bronx's Quiet, Brutal War With Opioids." *The New York Times*, 12 Oct. 2017, https://www.nytimes.com/2017/10/12/nyregion/bronx-heroin-fentanyl-opioid-overdoses.html.

FRIEDMAN, RICHARD A. "How Doctors Helped Drive the Addiction Crisis." *The New York Times*, 07 Nov. 2015, https://www.nytimes.com/2015/11/08/opinion/sunday/how-doctors-helped-drive-the-addiction-crisis.html.

GOODMAN, J. DAVID. "New York is a Hub in a Surging Heroin Trade." *The New York Times*, 19 May 2014, https://www.nytimes.com/2014/05/20/nyregion/new-york-is-a-hub-in-a-surging-heroin-trade.html.

GOODMAN, J. DAVID AND ANEMONA HORTOCOLLIS. "Anti-Overdose Drug Becoming An Everyday Part of Police Work." *The New York Times*, 12 June 2014, https://www.nytimes.com/2014/06/13/nyregion/anti-overdose-drug-becoming-an-everyday-part-of-police-work.html.

GOODNOUGH, ABBY. "White House Panel Recommends Declaring National Emergency On Opioids." *The New York Times*, 31 July 2017, https://www.nytimes.com/2017/07/31/health/opioid-crisis-trump-commission.html.

GOODNOUGH, ABBY AND KATE ZERNIKE. "Study Finds Competing Opioid Treatments Have Similar Outcomes." *The New York Times*, 14 Nov. 2017, https://www.nytimes.com/2017/11/14/health/vivitrol-suboxone-addiction-treatment.html.

HEALY, JACK. "Drug Linked to Ohio Overdoses Can Kill In Doses Smaller than a Snowflake." *The New York Times*, 05 Sept. 2016, https://www.nytimes.com/2016/09/06/us/ohio-cincinnati-overdoses-carfentanil-heroin.html.

KATZ, JOSH. "Drug Deaths In America Are Rising Faster Than Ever." *The New York Times*, 05 June 2017, https://www.nytimes.com/interactive/2017/06/05/upshot/opioid-epidemic-drug-overdose-deaths-are-rising-faster-than-ever.html.

KATZ, JOSH. "The First Count of Fentanyl Deaths in 2016: Up 540% in Three Years." *The New York Times*, 02 Sept. 2017, https://www.nytimes.com/interactive/2017/09/02/upshot/fentanyl-drug-overdose-deaths.html.

KATZ, JOSH, AND ABBY GOODNOUGH. "The Opioid Crisis Is Getting Worse, Particularly for Black Americans." *The New York Times*, 22 Dec. 2017, https://www.nytimes.com/interactive/2017/12/22/upshot/opioid-deaths-are-spreading-rapidly-into-black-america.html.

MEIER, BARRY. "Tightening The Lid On Pain Prescriptions." *The New York Times*, 08 April 2012, http://www.nytimes.com/2012/04/09/health/opioid

-painkiller-prescriptions-pose-danger-without-oversight.html.

THE NEW YORK TIMES. "Doctors Will Play a Critical Role in the Opioid Epidemic." *The New York Times*, 30 Aug. 2016, https://www.nytimes.com/2016/08/30/ opinion/doctors-will-play-a-critical-role-in-the-opioid-epidemic.html.

ROBLES, FRANCES. "Meth, the Forgotten Killer, Is Back. And It's Everywhere." *The New York Times*, 13 Feb. 2018, https://www.nytimes.com/2018/02/13/ us/meth-crystal-drug.html.

RUIZ, REBECCA. "Attorney General Orders Tougher Sentences, Rolling Back Obama Policy." *The New York Times*, 12 May 2017, https://www.nytimes .com/2017/05/12/us/politics/attorney-general-jeff-sessions-drug-offenses -penalties.html.

SEELYE, KATHARINE Q. "A Call to Arms on a Vermont Heroin Epidemic." *The New York Times*, 27 Feb. 2014, https://www.nytimes.com/2014/02/28/us/ a-call-to-arms-on-a-vermont-heroin-epidemic.html.

SEELYE, KATHARINE Q. "Heroin Epidemic Increasingly Seeps Into Public View." *The New York Times*, 06 March 2016, https://www.nytimes.com/2016/03/07/ us/heroin-epidemic-increasingly-seeps-into-public-view.html.

SEELYE, KATHARINE Q. "Heroin Scourge Overtakes a 'Quaint' Vermont Town." *The New York Times*, 05 March 2014, https://www.nytimes.com/2014/03/06/us/ bulwark-in-revolutionary-war-town-in-vermont-faces-heroin-scourge.html.

SEELYE, KATHARINE Q. "In Annual Speech, Vermont Governor Shifts Focus to Drug Abuse." *The New York Times*, 08 Jan. 2014, https://www.nytimes.com/ 2014/01/09/us/in-annual-speech-vermont-governor-shifts-focus-to-drug -abuse.html.

SEELYE, KATHARINE Q. "In Heroin Crisis, White Families Seek Gentler War on Drugs." *The New York Times*, 30 Oct. 2015, https://www.nytimes.com/2015/ 10/31/us/heroin-war-on-drugs-parents.html.

SEELYE, KATHARINE Q. "Naloxone Saves Lives, But Is No Cure In Heroin Epidemic." *The New York Times*, 27 July 2016, https://www.nytimes.com/ 2016/07/28/us/naloxone-eases-pain-of-heroin-epidemic-but-not-without -consequences.html.

SEELYE, KATHARINE Q. "Obituaries Shed Euphemisms to Chronicle Toll of Heroin." *The New York Times*, 11 July 2015, https://www.nytimes.com/2015/07/12/ us/obituaries-shed-euphemisms-to-confront-heroins-toll.html.

SEELYE, KATHARINE Q. AND ABBY GOODNOUGH. "Addiction Treatment Grew Under Health Law. Now What?" *The New York Times*, 10 Feb. 2017, https:// www.nytimes.com/2017/02/10/health/addiction-treatment-opiods-aca

-obamacare.html.

SMITH, MITCH AND MONICA DAVEY. "With Overdoses On Rise, Cities and Counties Look for Someone to Blame." *The New York Times*, 20 Dec. 2017, https://www.nytimes.com/2017/12/20/us/opioid-cities-counties-lawsuits.html.

SONTAG, DEBORAH. "At Clinics, Tumultuous Lives And Turbulent Care." *The New York Times*, 17 Nov. 2013, https://www.nytimes.com/2013/11/18/health/at-clinics-tumultuous-lives-and-turbulent-care.html.

TAVERNISE, SABRINA. "Ohio County Losing Its Young to Painkillers' Grip." *The New York Times*, 19 April 2011, http://www.nytimes.com/2011/04/20/us/20drugs.html.

TURKEWITZ, JULIE. " 'The Pills Are Everywhere': How the Opioid Crisis Claims Its Youngest Victims." *The New York Times*, 20 Sept. 2017, https://www.nytimes.com/2017/09/20/us/opioid-deaths-children.html.

WEE, SUI-LEE AND JAVIER C. HERNÁNDEZ. "Despite Trump's Pleas, China's Online Opioid Bazaar Is Booming." *The New York Times*, 08 Nov. 2017, https://www.nytimes.com/2017/11/08/world/asia/china-opioid-trump.html.

WILLIAMS, TIMOTHY. "This Judge Has a Mission: Keep Defendants Alive." *The New York Times*, 03 Jan. 2018, https://www.nytimes.com/2018/01/03/us/buffalo-heroin-opioid-court.html.

WILSON, MICHAEL. "A Death on Staten Island Highlight's Heroin's Place in 'Mainstream Society.' " *The New York Times*, 02 Oct. 2016, https://www.nytimes.com/2016/10/03/nyregion/a-death-on-staten-island-highlights-heroins-place-in-mainstream-society.html.

YEGINSU, CEYLAN. "Fentanyl Adds Deadly Kick to Opioid Woes in Britain." *The New York Times*, 04 Feb. 2018, https://www.nytimes.com/2018/02/04/world/europe/uk-fentanyl-opioid-addiction.html.

Index